Academic Language Mastery

Volumes in the
Academic Language Mastery Series

Series Editor: Ivannia Soto

Academic Language Mastery: Grammar and Syntax in Context
David E. Freeman, Yvonne S. Freeman, and Ivannia Soto

Academic Language Mastery: Conversational Discourse in Context
Jeff Zwiers and Ivannia Soto

Academic Language Mastery: Vocabulary in Context
Margarita Calderón and Ivannia Soto

Academic Language Mastery: Culture in Context
Noma LeMoine and Ivannia Soto

Academic Language Mastery:
Grammar and Syntax
in Context

David E. Freeman
Yvonne S. Freeman
Ivannia Soto

CORWIN
A SAGE Publishing Company

CORWIN
A SAGE Publishing Company

FOR INFORMATION:

Corwin

A SAGE Company

2455 Teller Road

Thousand Oaks, California 91320

(800) 233-9936

www.corwin.com

SAGE Publications Ltd.

1 Oliver's Yard

55 City Road

London EC1Y 1SP

United Kingdom

SAGE Publications India Pvt. Ltd.

B 1/I 1 Mohan Cooperative Industrial Area

Mathura Road, New Delhi 110 044

India

SAGE Publications Asia-Pacific Pte. Ltd.

3 Church Street

#10-04 Samsung Hub

Singapore 049483

Program Director: Dan Alpert

Senior Associate Editor: Kimberly Greenberg

Editorial Assistant: Katie Crilley

Production Editor: Amy Schroller

Copy Editor: Pam Schroeder

Typesetter: C&M Digitals (P) Ltd.

Proofreader: Dennis W. Webb

Indexer: Sheila Bodell

Cover Designer: Anupama Krishnan

Marketing Manager: Charline Maher

Printed in the United States of America

ISBN 978-1-5063-3716-6

This book is printed on acid-free paper.

SUSTAINABLE FORESTRY INITIATIVE

Certified Chain of Custody
Promoting Sustainable Forestry
www.sfiprogram.org
SFI-01268

SFI label applies to text stock

16 17 18 19 20 10 9 8 7 6 5 4 3 2 1

Contents

Acknowledgments

I would like to acknowledge each of the authors who coauthored this series with me: Margarita Calderón, David and Yvonne Freeman, Noma LeMoine, and Jeff Zwiers. I have been inspired by each of your work for so long, and it was an honor learning and working with you on this project. I know that this book series is stronger due to each of your contributions and will therefore affect the lives of so many English language learners (ELLs) and standard English learners (SELs). Thank you for taking this journey with me on behalf of students who need our collective voices!

I would also like to acknowledge my editor, Dan Alpert, who has believed in me and has supported my work since 2008. Thank you for tirelessly advocating for equity, including language equity, for so long! Thank you also for advocating for and believing in the vision of the Institute for Culturally and Linguistically Responsive Teaching (ICLRT)!

Also to be thanked is Corwin, for supporting my work over time as well as early contributions to ICLRT. Corwin has grown over the time that I published my first book in 2009, but they still remain a family. I would especially like to thank Michael Soule, Lisa Shaw, Kristin Anderson, Monique Corrdiori, Amelia Arias, Taryn Waters, Charline Maher, Kim Greenberg, and Katie Crilley for each of your parts in making this book series and ICLRT a success!

Last, I would like to acknowledge the California Community Foundation, whose two-year grant assisted greatly with fully launching ICLRT at Whittier College. Thank you for believing that effective professional development over time can and will create achievement and life changes for ELLs and SELs!

PUBLISHER'S ACKNOWLEDGMENTS

Corwin gratefully acknowledges the contributions of the following reviewers:

Bridget Erickson
Teacher, Literacy Specialist
Oakwood Elementary School, Wayzata Public Schools
Plymouth, MN

Sara Hamerla
ELL Coach
Barbieri Elementary School
Framingham, MA

Katherine Lobo
ESL Teacher, President of MATSOL
Newton South High School
Newton, MA

Sashi Rayasam
Educator
Durham Public Schools
Durham, NC

Renee Sartore
Director of ELL Programs
Yorkville CUSD 115
Yorkville, IL

Tonya Ward Singer
Author and Consultant
Santa Rosa, CA

About the Authors

 **Dr. David E. Freeman** and **Dr. Yvonne S. Freeman** are professors emeriti at the University of Texas Río Grande Valley. Both are interested in effective education for emergent bilinguals. They present regularly at international, national, and state conferences. They have worked extensively in schools in the United States. They have also worked with educators in Ecuador, Mexico, Colombia, Venezuela, Costa Rica, Argentina, Uruguay, Hong Kong, India, Indonesia, Lithuania, Mallorca, Taiwan, and Sweden. In 2016 they worked in Taiwan.

The Freemans have published books, articles, and book chapters jointly and separately on the topics of second language teaching, biliteracy, bilingual education, linguistics, and second language acquisition. Their newest books are *ESL Teaching: Principles for Success* (2016) and *Essential Linguistics: What Teachers Need to Know to Teach ESL, Reading, Spelling, and Grammar*, 2nd edition (2014), published by Heinemann. The Freemans also edited two research publications published by EmeraldBooks: *Research on Preparing Pre-Service Teachers to Work Effectively With Emergent Bilinguals* and *Research on Preparing In-Service Teachers to Work Effectively With Emergent Bilinguals*. They also edited *Diverse Learners in the Mainstream Classroom* (2008), published by Heinemann.

Other books written by the Freemans and published by Heinemann include *Between Worlds: Access to Second Language Acquisition*, 3rd edition (2011); *Academic Language for English Language Learners and Struggling Readers* (2009); the revised translation of *La enseñanza de la lectura y la escritura en español y en inglés en clases bilingües y de doble inmersión* (2009); the second edition of *Teaching Reading and Writing in Spanish and English in Bilingual and Dual Language Classrooms* (2006); *Dual Language Essentials for Teachers and Administrators* (2005); *Closing the Achievement Gap: How to Reach Limited Formal Schooling and Long-Term English Learners* (2002); *Teaching Reading in Multilingual Classrooms* (2000); and *ESL/EFL Teaching: Principles for Success* (1998).

The Freemans are authors on Houghton Mifflin Harcourt's programs *On Our Way to English* and *Literacy by Design* as well as Benchmark Education's Spanish reading program.

Dr. Ivannia Soto is associate professor of education at Whittier College, where she specializes in second language acquisition, systemic reform for ELLs, and urban education. She began her career in the Los Angeles Unified School District (LAUSD), where she taught English and English language development to a population made of up 99.9 percent Latinos, who either were or had been ELLs. Before becoming a professor, Dr. Soto also served LAUSD as a literacy coach and district office administrator. She has presented on literacy and language topics at various conferences, including the National Association for Bilingual Education (NABE), the California Association for Bilingual Education (CABE), the American Educational Research Association (AERA), and the National Urban Education Conference. As a consultant, Soto has worked with Stanford University's School Redesign Network (SRN) and WestEd as well as a variety of districts and county offices in California, providing technical assistance for systemic reform for ELLs and Title III. Soto is the coauthor of *The Literacy Gaps: Building Bridges for ELLs and SELs* as well as author of *ELL Shadowing as a Catalyst for Change* and *From Spoken to Written Language with ELLs*, all published by Corwin. Together, the books tell a story of how to systemically close achievement gaps with ELLs by increasing their oral language production in academic areas. Soto is executive director of the Institute for Culturally and

Linguistically Responsive Teaching (ICLRT) at Whittier College, whose mission it is to promote relevant research and develop academic resources for ELLs and SELs via linguistically and culturally responsive teaching practices.

Series Dedication

I dedicate this book series to the teachers and administrators in Whittier Union High School District (WUHSD). WUHSD has been a pivotal learning partner with ICLRT over the past four years. By embedding ICLRT Design Principles and academic language development (ALD) best practices into their teaching and professional development, they have fully embraced and worked tirelessly in classrooms to meet the needs of ELLs and SELs. Specifically, I would like to thank: Superintendent Sandy Thorstenson, Assistant Superintendent Loring Davies, and ELL Director Lilia Torres-Cooper (my high school counselor and the person who initially brought me into WUHSD) as well as ALD Certification teachers Diana Banzet, Amy Cantrell, Carlos Contreras, Carmen Telles Fox, Nellie Garcia, Kristin Kowalsky, Kelsey McDonnell, Damian Torres, and Heather Vernon, who have committed themselves fully to this work. I would also like to thank Lori Eshilian, principal of Whittier High School (my high school alma mater), for being willing to do whatever it takes to meet the needs of all students, including partnering with ICLRT on several projects over the past few years. You were my first and best physical education teacher and have modeled effective collaboration since I was in high school!

—Ivannia Soto, Series Editor

Book Dedication

For teachers who often are not sure how to teach grammar effectively and students who find grammar either boring or irrelevant.

—David E. Freeman and Yvonne S. Freeman

CHAPTER ONE

Introduction to the Book Series

According to the Migration Policy Institute (2013), close to 5 million U.S. students, which represent 9 percent of public school enrollment, are English language learners (ELLs). Three-quarters of these 5 million students were born in the United States and are either the children or grandchildren of immigrants. In some large urban school districts such as Los Angeles, ELLs already comprise around 30 percent of the student population. These demographic trends, along with the rigorous content expectations of new content and language standards (e.g., CCSS, WIDA, ELPA21, etc.), require that educational systems become skilled at simultaneously scaffolding academic language and content for this growing group of students. For ELLs, academic language mastery is the key to accessing rigorous content. Now is a pivotal time in educational history to address both academic language and content simultaneously so that ELLs do not fall further behind in both areas while also becoming bored by methods that are cognitively banal and lead to disengagement.

Another group of students who have academic language needs, but are not formally identified as such, are standard English learners (SELs). SELs are students who speak languages that do not correspond to standard American English language structure and grammar but incorporate English vocabulary. They include African American students who speak African American language

(AAL), sometimes referred to as African American English, and Mexican American–non-new-immigrant students who speak Mexican American Language (MxAL) or what is commonly referred to as "Chicano English." ELLs and SELS also need instructional assistance in the academic language necessary to be successful in school, college, and beyond. For both groups of students, academic language represents the pathway to full access in meeting the rigorous demands of the new standards.

PURPOSE OF THIS ACADEMIC LANGUAGE DEVELOPMENT BOOK SERIES

The purpose of this series is to assist educators in developing expertise in, and practical strategies for, addressing four key dimensions of academic language when working with ELLs and SELs. To systemically address the needs of ELLs and SELs, we educators must share a common understanding of academic language development (ALD). Wong-Fillmore (2013) defines academic language as "the language of texts. The forms of speech and written discourse that are linguistic resources educated people in our society can draw on. This is language that is capable of supporting complex thought, argumentation, literacy, successful learning; it is the language used in written and spoken communication in college and beyond" (p. 15). Given that we are preparing ELLs and SELs for college, career, and beyond, they should receive ample opportunities to learn and use academic language, both in spoken and written form (Soto, 2014). ELLs and SELs also must be provided with scaffolded access to cognitively and linguistically demanding content, which allows them to cultivate their complex thinking and argumentation.

All students can benefit from academic language development modeling, scaffolding, and practice, but ELLs and SELs need it to survive and thrive in school. ELLs have plenty of language assets in their primary language that we must leverage to grow their academic English, yet there is often a very clear language and literacy gap that must be closed as soon as ELLs enter school. Similarly, SELs come to school with a language variation that, to be built upon in the classroom setting, must first be understood. In reviewing the wide range of literature by experts in this field, most agree that the key elements of academic English language for ELLs and SELs include these four dimensions: academic vocabulary, syntax and grammar, discourse, and culturally responsive teaching.

We have therefore organized this book series around these four dimensions of academic English:

- Conversational Discourse—developing students' conversational skills as an avenue for fostering academic language and thinking in a discipline
- Academic Vocabulary—teaching high-frequency academic words and discipline-specific vocabulary across content areas
- Syntax and Grammar—teaching sophisticated and complex syntactical and grammatical structures in context
- Responsive Teaching—incorporating culture while addressing and teaching language and honoring students' home cultures and communities

The focus on these four dimensions in this book series makes this a unique offering for educators. By building upon the cultural and linguistic similarities of ELLs and SELs, we embed strategies and instructional approaches about academic vocabulary, discourse, and grammar and syntax within culturally responsive teaching practices to make them all accessible to teachers of diverse students. As the American poet and great thinker of modern Hispanic literature, Sabine Ulibarrí, noted, "Language is culture; it carries with it traditions, customs, the very life of a people. You cannot separate one from the other. To love one is to love the other; to hate one is to hate the other. If one wants to destroy a people, take away their language and their culture will soon disappear." Therefore, the heart of this book series is to integrate language and culture in a manner that has not been addressed with other books or book series on ALD.

ACADEMIC LANGUAGE DEVELOPMENT DIMENSIONS DEFINED AND CONNECTIONS TO THE BOOK SERIES

ALD is a pathway to equity. With new, rigorous state standards and expectations, ALD is the scaffold that provides access for ELLs and SELs so that high academic expectations can be maintained and reached. The following matrix defines each dimension of ALD and demonstrates the connection of that ALD dimension across the book series. For full proficiency in ALD, it is integral that each dimension be addressed across disciplines—the dimensions should not be taught as either/or skills. Instead, each of the dimensions should be addressed throughout a course of study or unit. In that way, it is important to read the book series in its entirety, as an ongoing professional development growth tool (more on that later). The matrix also demonstrates the connections made between ALD dimensions, which will prove helpful as readers complete continue their study across the ALD book series.

ALD Dimension	Definition	Connections to the Book Series
Academic Discourse	Academic discourse is putting words and sentences (the other two dimensions) together to clearly communicate complex ideas. The essential components of academic discourse include: • Message organization and text structure • Voice and register • Density of words, sentences, and ideas • Clarity and coherence • Purpose, functions, and audience	As suggested in the definition, academic discourse involves the overlap of academic vocabulary (words) and many of the components also often associated with academic writing across genres (organization, text structure, purpose, and audience). This book addresses a specific form of discourse, conversational discourse, and the specific conversational skills that provide access to academic discourse.
Academic Vocabulary	Words are separate units of information; it is tempting to focus on them as "pieces of knowledge" to accumulate to show learning. Instead, words should be tools and materials for constructing more complete and complex messages. In this book series, we will focus on Tier 2	Academic vocabulary is associated with the density of words used in academic discourse as well as the use of connectives and transitions used in grammar.

ALD Dimension	Definition	Connections to the Book Series
	(high-frequency words that go across content areas) and Tier 3 (abstract or nuanced words that exist within a particular content area or discipline) academic vocabulary.	
Grammar and Syntax in Context	Academic language is characterized by technical vocabulary, lexical density, and abstraction. Academic genres have predictable components, cohesive texts, and language structures that include nominalizations, passives, and complex sentences.	ELLs and SELs need to engage in academic discourse in the classroom and develop academic vocabulary. These are essential building blocks for learning to read and write cohesive texts using academic genres and the language structures characteristic of academic language.
Culturally and Linguistically Responsive Practices	Culturally responsive pedagogy incorporates high-status, accurate cultural knowledge about different ethnic groups into all subjects and skills taught. It validates, facilitates, liberates, and empowers ethnically diverse students by simultaneously cultivating their cultural integrity, individual abilities, and academic success (Gay, 2000).	ELLs and SELs are more likely to acquire ALD when they are viewed from an asset model and when ALD is taught as associated with concepts that connect to their cultural knowledge. This book will address linguistic diversity, including variations of English.

(Definitions adapted from Academic Language Development Network. (n.d.) *unless otherwise noted)*

FORMAT FOR EACH BOOK

At the beginning of each book is an introduction to the purpose of the book series, including the format of each book and their intersections. Additionally, connections between current ALD research and the specific dimension of ALD are included in an abbreviated literature review. In the middle of each book, the voice of the expert in the particular ALD dimension is incorporated with practical strategies and classroom examples. These chapters include how to move from theory to practice, classroom examples at elementary and secondary levels, and ways to assess the dimension. At the end of each book, a summary of major points and how to overcome related challenges are included along with the rationale for use of the Institute for Culturally and Linguistically Responsive Teaching (ICLRT) Design Principles as a bridge between ALD and content. Also included at the end of each book are additional professional development resources.

Additionally, each book in the series is organized in a similar manner for ease of use by the reader. Chapter 1 is the introduction to the series of books and not an introduction for each individual book. Instead, Chapter 2 introduces each dimension of ALD with the specific research base for that book. The heart of each book in the series is in Chapter 3, where practical application to theory and classroom examples can be found. Chapter 4 addresses how each ALD dimension fosters literacy development. In Chapter 5, how to assess the specific ALD dimension is discussed with checklists and rubrics to assist with formative assessment in this area. Last, Chapter 6 connects each volume with the others in the series and details how the book series can best be used in a professional development setting. The epilogue revisits the vision for the series and provides a description of the relationship to the underlying principles of the ICLRT.

- Chapter 1—Introduction to the Book Series
- Chapter 2—Abbreviated Literature Review/Research Base for Grammar and Syntax
- Chapter 3— Practical Application to the Classroom for Grammar and Syntax
- Chapter 4—Fostering Literacy With Grammar and Syntax
- Chapter 5— Assessing Grammar and Syntax
- Chapter 6—Conclusions, Challenges, and Connections
- Epilogue: The Vision

How to Use the Book Series

While each book can stand alone, the book series was designed to be read together with colleagues and over time. As such, it is a professional development tool for educational communities, which can also be used for extended learning on ALD. Educators may choose to begin with any of the four key dimensions of ALD that interests them the most or with which they need the most assistance.

How to Use Reflect and Apply Queries

Embedded throughout this book series you will find queries that will ask you to reflect and apply new learning to your own practice. Please note that you may choose to use the queries in a variety of settings either with a book study buddy during PLC, grade-level, or department meetings. Each of the queries can be answered in a separate journal while one is reading the text, or as a group you may choose to reflect on only a few queries throughout a chapter. Please feel free to use as many or as few queries as are helpful to you, but we do encourage you to at least try a couple out for reflection as you read the book series.

Try it out by responding to the first query here.

REFLECT AND APPLY

What does the following Sabine Ulibarrí quote mean to you? How does it connect to your students?

"Language is culture; it carries with it traditions, customs, the very life of a people. You cannot separate one from the other. To love one is to love the other; to hate one is to hate the other. If one wants to destroy a people, take away their language and their culture will soon disappear."

Book Series Connection to Grammar and Syntax

As previously discussed, grammar and syntax are essential components of ALD. Unfortunately, these components have either been overly emphasized and some teachers have taught grammar in a rote manner that is decontextualized and disconnected to student needs and learning, or they have completely disregarded grammar due to their lack of experience in teaching grammar and syntax appropriately. Still other teachers become overwhelmed with the large gaps in the knowledge of grammar and syntax that ELLs may bring to school and are unsure of the best approaches to meeting students' needs. This book on grammar and syntax addresses these concerns, first by building background knowledge and confidence on the part of educators regarding the varying views of grammar that have been used and then by giving specific recommendations for how to teach ALD in a contextualized manner that addresses ELLs' and SELs' language gaps. The approach to teaching grammar and syntax introduced in this book in the series, along with the ICLRT Design Principles (in the epilogue), provide a theoretical and practical framework for addressing ALD in a contextualized manner across disciplines.

CHAPTER TWO

Abbreviated Literature Review/Research Base for Grammar and Syntax

To understand the role of grammar and syntax in ALD, it is important to have a clear understanding of the terms *grammar* and *syntax* as well as an understanding of the characteristics of academic language. Teachers who understand these concepts can better plan how to teach and assess English language learners.

FOUR VIEWS OF GRAMMAR

In the minds of most people, grammar refers to a set of rules needed to speak and write the standard or conventional form of a language. A second view is that grammar is the built-in, subconscious knowledge of a language that enables people to communicate in that language. Most linguists, especially those whose work is based on Chomsky's (1965) theories, consider grammar to be the study of syntactic structures. For these linguists the terms *grammar* and *syntax* are synonymous. More recently systemic functional linguists have developed a theory of grammar as a functional resource.

Weaver (1996) lists these definitions of grammar: (1) prescriptions for correct use, (2) the functional command of sentence structure that enables us to comprehend and produce language, and (3) a description of syntactic structures. Derewianka (2007) adds a fourth view in her explanation of language as a functional resource. Each of these views of grammar has led to different approaches to teaching ELLs and SELs the grammar and syntax of academic language.

PRESCRIPTIONS FOR CORRECT USE

For most people, the word *grammar* means studying rules for correct speaking and writing. At one time schools were conducted in Latin. Teachers in these grammar schools taught Latin grammar. When the language of instruction shifted to English, these same teachers applied their knowledge of Latin grammar to English and began to teach English grammar. Because students could already understand and speak English, the focus was on written language. Teachers believed that their job was to prescribe the rules of the language, and if students learned grammar, they could apply this knowledge to both writing and speaking.

REFLECT AND APPLY

What was your own experience with being taught grammar when you were in school? Did you find grammar interesting or frustrating? Be prepared to share with your colleagues.

RESEARCH ON THE EFFECTS OF TEACHING TRADITIONAL GRAMMAR

Despite the widespread practice of teaching formal grammar explicitly, research has consistently shown that students have trouble learning traditional grammar or applying grammar rules when they write or speak. In the first place, students find it difficult to learn and retain concepts from traditional grammar. In one series of studies, Macauley (1947) tested the grammar knowledge of students in schools in Scotland. At the time of these studies, grammar was taught in both elementary and secondary schools for an average of 30 minutes a day. At the elementary level, the lessons emphasized knowing parts of speech and their functions. For example, students were taught to identify nouns in a sentence, and they learned that nouns served as subjects and objects.

Macauley tested students at the end of elementary school. The test required students to read 50 sentences and decide whether the underlined word in each sentence was a noun, verb, pronoun, adjective, or adverb. Even though all the students had studied the parts of speech every day for several years, the average score for the 131 students was a mere 27.9 percent right. Macauley had set 50 as a passing score. Students could get about 11 percent right just by guessing, but only one student scored 50 percent or better on all five parts of speech.

When Macauley tested secondary students, they did somewhat better, but the mean for the top classes at the end of their third year of secondary school had only risen to 62 percent. Macauley's studies with students who received intensive training in traditional grammar showed that students have a great deal of difficulty even learning basic parts of speech.

Krashen (1998) also reviewed research on the teaching of grammar. His conclusion is blunt: "Research on the relationship between formal grammar instruction and performance on measures of writing ability is very consistent: There is no relationship between grammar study and writing" (p. 8).

One of the strongest statements on the teaching of grammar comes from a report issued by the National Council of Teachers of English, an organization with many members vitally interested in grammar and in the teaching of writing. The authors of the report state:

> In view of the widespread agreement of research studies based upon many types of students and teachers, the conclusion can be stated in strong and unqualified terms: the teaching of formal grammar has a negligible or, because it usually displaces some instruction and practice in actual composition, even a harmful effect on the improvement of writing. (Braddock & Lloyd-Jones, 1963)

None of these are new studies. There are no current studies that dispute the early findings. Despite the research consensus, teachers continue to teach traditional grammar to native standard English speakers, SELs, and ELLs. Weaver (1996) lists several reasons:

- Teachers may not be aware of the research.
- They may not believe the research.
- They believe grammar is interesting and teach it simply for that reason.
- They notice that some students who are good readers and writers are also good at grammar, so they assume that this correlation shows cause and effect.
- They are required to teach grammar.
- They feel pressure from parents or other community members to teach grammar.
- They feel that although grammar may not help the average student, it still may help some students.

REFLECT AND APPLY

Have you taught grammar to your students? Did you find that the students learned from your grammar teaching? Do any of the reasons that teachers still teach traditional grammar apply to you or to your colleagues?

TRADITIONAL GRAMMAR AND ENGLISH LANGUAGE TEACHING

Teachers do need to know about grammar. This should be part of their pedagogical language knowledge (Bunch, 2013). However, teachers should not expect that teaching traditional grammar will improve their students' academic language proficiency.

Derewianka (2007) refers to the traditional approach to teaching grammar as "language as structure." This approach involves identifying different parts of speech, such as nouns and verbs, and the rules for combining them into sentences. As Derewianka writes, "Traditionally grammar in the ELT [English language teaching] field has been conceived of in terms of identifying the parts of speech and the rules for combining them intro structures" (2007, p. 844). *Structures* refers to subjects, predicates, and other parts of a sentence. Traditional approaches to second language teaching, such as the Grammar Translation method, used this approach. This method consists of explicit teaching of rules followed by decontextualized exercises designed to give students practice with the rule. For example, students might learn the proper forms for the present perfect tense in English and then be given an exercise in which they convert past tense sentences, such as "He studied English," to present perfect, "He has studied English."

Derewianka (2007) comments that a traditional approach to teaching grammar is still the most widely used model of English language teaching. However, this applies primarily to teaching English in countries where English is not the native language. Traditional approaches to grammar teaching result in students learning about the language (they can tell you how to form the present perfect tense), but this approach has not been shown to help students develop the ability to communicate in the language. As a result, in English as a second language (as opposed to English as a foreign language) and bilingual classes, traditional grammar is not usually taught.

Focus on Form

Although traditional grammar-based approaches to teaching a second language are outdated and are not supported by research, within more current second language teaching methods, some aspects of grammar continue to be taught. That is, there is still what Long (2001) refers to as a "focus on form."

Ellis (1998) looked at three ways of presenting form-focused instruction. One way is to structure the input. "This option asks learners to process input that has been specially contrived to induce comprehension of the target structure" (p. 44). Learners are not required to produce the structure, but they are exposed to large amounts of the structure and asked to attend to it. For example, students often say things like "I am boring" when they mean, "I am bored," so structured input might focus on the difference between these two grammatical forms. For example, the teacher might give students a reading that contains many examples of "boring" and "bored" and similar pairs that students often confuse.

To take another example, the teacher could ask students what they would do if they won the lottery. The teacher might give the example: "If I won the lottery, I would buy my parents a new house." Then the teacher could have each student report on what he or she would do. As they listen to these examples, all the students would receive input that contained the conditional structure: "If I ___, I would ___."

A second possibility that Ellis suggests is explicit instruction. Such instruction can be direct (the teacher teaches the rule, and the students practice it) or indirect. In indirect explicit instruction, students look at some sample of language and try to figure out the rule. Explicit instruction can be deductive or inductive. Explicit instruction is designed to raise students' consciousness of the grammatical form.

An example of indirect explicit instruction might involve students looking at a series of phrases that each contains several adjectives before a noun, such as, "a large heavy brown leather English suitcase." Based on their analyses of the phrases, students could develop a rule for the order of adjectives preceding a noun. Native English speakers recognize that it does not seem right to change the order and say, "a brown heavy English leather large suitcase." Once students develop a rule, they can test it against new noun phrases with several adjectives.

A third approach to incorporating grammar into second language teaching is what Ellis (1998) calls "production practice." This approach involves students in practicing certain grammatical forms. For example, students might do a worksheet that asks them to put the words *in*, *on*, or *at* into the appropriate blanks in a sentence. Finally, teachers can teach grammar by providing negative feedback. When a student makes an error, the teacher can correct it, usually by modeling the correct form. For instance, if the student says, "I have been here since two days," the teacher might respond, "Oh, so you have been here *for* two days. What have you been doing?" As Ellis points out, most language teaching includes a combination of these methods, so it is difficult to know which one works best.

REFLECT AND APPLY

Which type of grammar instruction have you experienced as a student? Have you taught grammar to students using one or a combination of the four approaches to teaching grammar described in this chapter?

THE FUNCTIONAL COMMAND
OF SENTENCE STRUCTURE

A second view of grammar is that a grammar is a set of internalized rules that people acquire. These are the rules that allow humans to communicate in a language. Derewianka refers to this view as "language as mental faculty." Chomsky (1965) and other linguists argue that humans have an innate capacity for language. We are born with Universal Grammar, a set of mental structures that enable us to use language input to form subconscious rules to understand and produce one or more languages. The internal grammar includes a syntactic component along with knowledge of phonology, morphology, semantics, and pragmatics. Over time, humans develop a full command of the grammar of their community of speakers, and this allows them to function effectively.

Chomsky (1975) argues that humans have an innate ability to construct rules that allow them to comprehend and produce utterances in any language. What they need is exposure to specific languages to refine general rules to fit those languages. Given that this is a subconscious process that functions without the need for teaching of the rules, this view of language leads to a belief that explicit grammar teaching is not necessary for language acquisition. Clearly, no one teaches babies grammar rules, and yet they acquire language.

For second language teaching, the basic question is whether second language learners can still acquire language the same way that children acquire their first language. Sociolinguists such as Grosjean (2010) provide numerous examples of how adolescents and adults can acquire a second language. Krashen's (1982) theory of second language acquisition is based on Chomsky's theory of language. He argues that a second language can be acquired in the same way as a first language by receiving comprehensible input.

Krashen has written extensively about the value of reading as a source of comprehensible input. He has developed a reading hypothesis. Krashen (1992) states:

> Current theories of literacy development hypothesize that we develop literacy the same way we acquire language, by means of comprehensible input. Smith (1988a) and Goodman (1982) have presented compelling evidence that we "learn to read by reading," by making sense of what is on the page.

In addition, there is overwhelming evidence showing that free reading is the major source of our competence in many aspects of literacy, including vocabulary, spelling, grammatical competence, and writing style. (p. 8)

Using Grammar to Monitor Output

Within Krashen's theory, the benefits of grammar teaching are limited. However, Krashen explains that knowledge of grammar can be used to monitor output. Monitoring requires that the person knows the rule and has time to apply it. During conversations, it is difficult to monitor output because a person can't focus on meaning and grammatical correctness at the same time. If someone is trying to decide which endings go on verbs, that person can't also be thinking about the message he or she is trying to convey.

Yvonne remembers a time when she applied her monitor to her output. During her oral exams for her doctoral degree, one committee member asked her a question in Spanish. Yvonne knew that this was a setting where grammatical correctness would be expected. As she answered, she consciously thought about the rule in Spanish that says after expressions like "It is necessary," the subjunctive form of the verb must follow. She applied the rule as she was giving her answer in Spanish.

Immediately after the exam, a colleague from the Spanish department saw her and asked her how it went. As Yvonne excitedly told her about the exam and the positive feedback she received, she spoke in Spanish, but she did not apply her monitor once. She could well have made a few grammatical errors while speaking Spanish in this setting, but her focus was on explaining that she had passed the exam and had done well. Effective use of the monitor requires that speakers use it in appropriate contexts and do not overuse it or underuse it.

While applying the grammar rules may not always be practical when one is speaking, students should apply rules to monitor their writing. As we write, we usually have time to think about what we are writing, and we usually try to convey a clear message with as few errors as possible. When ELLs or SELs are provided short mini lessons on specific points of grammar they are having trouble with and then are given opportunities to edit papers working with the teacher and with peers, they begin to learn conventional English.

REFLECT AND APPLY

Have you ever been in a situation where you knew you needed to apply your monitor as you were speaking? What was the context? Were you able to monitor your grammatical correctness?

In our experience, students who are better writers are those who have done a great deal of reading. Do you think that reading can help people become better writers, that is, writers who write well grammatically? Can you think of some examples? Why might reading help students write well grammatically?

A DESCRIPTION OF SYNTACTIC STRUCTURES

A third view is that grammar is a description of syntactic structures. Although linguists study all the different aspects of language, the major area of study in recent years in the United States has been syntax, the structure of clauses. Syntax is one component of the grammar of a language. In their study of syntax, linguists have attempted to make explicit the implicit rules that humans have acquired that allow them to comprehend and produce language. Chomsky (1965) argued that there must be a small set of rules that can generate an infinite number of sentences. If there were a large set of rules, people could not acquire them.

Surface and Deep Structure

To create a small set of rules, Chomsky hypothesized that language has a surface structure and a deep structure. The surface structure is what we say or write—the sounds we make and the marks on a page. The deep structure is the underlying structure that is in basic form. Deep structures can be transformed to create different surface structures. Structural linguists attempted to describe language by using the surface structure outputs of speech and writing. However, these descriptions were very complex. Chomsky, in contrast, used deep structures as a basis for his descriptions. For example, Chomsky assumed that positive statements were basic, so they were considered the deep structure form, and questions and negative statements were surface structure variations.

This approach enabled Chomsky to identify basic syntactic structures for English. For example, a simple sentence (a clause) consists of a noun phrase, an auxiliary verb, and a verb phrase, and each type of phrase can be further described. A verb phrase contains a verb and can include one or more noun phrases, an adverb phrase, and a prepositional phrase. In early studies, using a theory of transformational, generative grammar, Chomsky attempted to describe how deep structures were transformed into surface structures. For instance, the statement, "He can play the tuba" can be converted into the question: "Can he play the tuba?" by moving the auxiliary to the left of the subject. In later work, Chomsky focused more on describing what limits movement of deep structure sentence elements rather than on describing each movement.

Chomsky's work provided important insights into syntactic structures. As he developed his theory of transformational grammar, articles and books on using transformational grammar to teach English were produced. However, attempts to teach ELLs or SELs conventional English by using insights from transformational grammar were not successful, and Chomsky's later work was not used as a basis for teaching language.

LANGUAGE AS FUNCTIONAL RESOURCE

Derewianka (2007) discusses a fourth view of grammar that she refers to as language as functional resource. This approach is based on linguistic studies by Halliday (1989) and his colleagues. Derewianka points out an important difference between Chomsky and Halliday. As she comments, Halliday explains language "not in terms of a genetic blueprint located in the individual brain, but as the result of countless social interactions over the millennia" (p. 849). Halliday sees language use as a series of choices based on the context of situation, which is made up of three components: the field (what we are talking about), the tenor (who we are talking to), and the mode (the means of communication, such as speech or writing). We constantly make choices in each of these areas to carry out social functions, such as explaining or describing. Each context of situation occurs in a context of culture as different cultural groups have different ways of carrying out the functions of language.

REFLECT AND APPLY

Think about how you talk in two different settings. For example, you might consider the conversation at the family dinner table and the conversation around the table at a formal banquet with other professionals. That is, think about the vocabulary you use and the formality of the language you use. How is the language you use different in the two settings? Why?

The Curriculum Cycle

In Australia, Halliday's approach to linguistics has been translated into a method of second language teaching called the curriculum cycle or the Teaching and Learning Cycle. The cycle involves building up the field (providing students with basic concepts for a subject or building background), modeling and deconstruction (e.g., showing students a model science report and analyzing the report so that students understand each part), joint construction (e.g., students and teacher work together to write a science report), and independent construction (students work independently to write their own science reports). The focus of this approach is to teach students the different academic genres, such as reports, analyses, and explanations.

CHARACTERISTICS OF ACADEMIC LANGUAGE

The challenge of teaching language to ELLs and SELs is greater now than it was in the past. Whereas earlier approaches to teaching ELLs and SELs, such as the Natural Approach (Krashen & Terrell, 1983) and ALM (Larsen-Freeman, 1986), focus on developing conversational language, more recent methods have shifted to an emphasis on academic language, even at beginning stages. In the course of their schooling, students are expected to read, write, and discuss texts written in the academic genres used in literature, science, social studies, and math. A text is any oral or written use of language. Academic texts are the oral and written texts used in schools (Freeman & Freeman, 2009).

Fang (2004) points out that academic texts are characterized by technical vocabulary, lexical density, and abstraction. These characteristics create an authoritative tone. The following passage from a high school physics and chemistry textbook is a good example of an academic text with these characteristics:

> Although fossil fuels are a useful source of energy for generating electricity and providing the power for transportation, their use has some undesirable side effects. When petroleum products and coal are burned, smoke is given off that contains small particles called particulates. These particulates cause breathing problems for some people. Burning fossil fuels also releases carbon dioxide. Figure 9 shows how the carbon dioxide concentration in the atmosphere has increased from 1960 to 1999. (McLaughlin, Thompson, & Zike, 2002, p. 296)

Technical Vocabulary and Lexical Density

This passage contains technical vocabulary, such as *particulates* and *concentration*. It also is lexically dense. Academic texts have greater density than conversational texts. Linguists measure lexical density by determining the number of lexical words in each clause. Lexical words are content words—nouns, verbs, adjectives, and some adverbs. This passage has 6.4 content words in each clause, whereas conversational language has about 2.5 content words per clause. Greater lexical density makes academic texts more cognitively demanding because more ideas are packed into each sentence.

Nominalization

Lexical density is often the result of long noun phrases. In this passage, the noun phrase "the carbon dioxide concentration in the atmosphere" has seven words. Frequently, long noun phrases result from nominalizations. Nominalization is the process of turning verbs or adjectives into nouns. In this passage, phrases such as "generating electricity and providing the power for transportation" and "Burning fossil fuels" contain nominalizations. Rather than saying, "Fossil fuels generate electricity and provide the power for transportation," the authors use the nominalized forms "generating" and "providing." Nominalizations are very common in academic texts. Consider the following two lists of words:

Verb or Adjective	Noun
introduce	introduction
honest	honesty
refuse	refusal
complex	complexity
create	creation
treat	treatment
toxic	toxicity

Now consider these sentences:

The scientist introduced his speech with a specific example. This made the audience more attentive.	The introduction of the scientist's speech with a specific example gained the audience's attention.
The main character in the novel was an honest man. This was his outstanding trait.	The main character's honesty was his outstanding trait.
Washington's soldiers refused to give up hope, even under difficult conditions. As a result they won the battle.	Washington's soldiers' refusal to give up hope, even under difficult conditions, led to their victory.
The calculus problem was very complex. Even the best students became frustrated.	The complexity of the calculus problem that the teacher had assigned frustrated even the best students.
The scientist mixed these two chemicals to create a compound.	The creation of this compound was the result of mixing these two chemicals.
The soldiers treated the prisoners humanely. This was noted in the report.	The soldier's humane treatment of the prisoners was noted in the report.
The gas was toxic. The workers began gasping.	The toxicity of the gas left the workers gasping.

Nominalization in these examples results in greater lexical density. When verbs and adjectives are turned into nouns, the nouns can become part of a complex noun phrase, as is shown in the second set of sentences in the table. For example, changing the verb *introduce* into the noun *introduction* results in a noun phrase with 10 words, as shown in the first example. The other examples are similar. These long noun phrases that are typical of academic writing are difficult for SELs and ELLs to understand or produce.

Teaching Nominalization

Secondary students can learn to incorporate nominalization into their writing with focused instruction. The first step would be for the teacher to give students a list of verbs and adjectives and ask them to convert these words into nouns. To help students do this, a teacher could give students a list of suffixes that are used to change verbs and adjectives into nouns, such as –tion (destroy, destruction), –ness (happy, happiness), –al (dismiss, dismissal).

When students understand nominalization, they can rewrite sentences that have nominalizations as simple sentences with adjectives and verbs. Later, students could begin to write their own sentences with nominalizations. Lessons on nominalization would be for advanced level ELLs and SELs.

Abstraction

Academic texts are also more abstract than conversational texts. Nominalizations make texts more abstract. Normally, speakers or writers communicate ideas in a concrete way. The syntax reflects the way we experience events. For example, when we say, "The soldiers treated the prisoners humanely," the order of the words follows the common subject-verb-object pattern. English speakers expect sentences to follow this pattern of actor, action, and thing acted on. That is, someone does something to someone or something. However, when the verb is turned into a noun, the result is a long noun phrase, "The soldiers' humane treatment of the prisoners" that expresses an abstract idea rather than describing an action.

In the passage about fossil fuels, nominalizations also make the text more abstract. If we write, "When people burn fossil fuels, the process releases carbon dioxide into the atmosphere." the result is a concrete sentence. Someone does something with a certain result. However, by using the nominalized form "Burning fossil fuels," the authors make this an abstract concept with no people involved.

The use of passives also makes academic texts abstract. The passage on fossil fuels contains several passives, such as "When petroleum products and coal are burned, smoke is given off that contains small particles called particulates." This is much more abstract than a sentence like, "When people burn petroleum products and coal, the process creates smoke that contains small particles called particulates." In active sentences the grammatical subject is the person or thing that does the action, but in a passive sentence, the grammatical subject is acted upon rather than being the one acting. If we say "People burn coal and petroleum products," the grammatical subject, "people," is the actor, but in the passive construction, "Petroleum products and coal are burned," the grammatical subject, "petroleum products and coal" it having something done to it. They are not acting but being acted on, and the result is a more abstract construction.

FEATURES OF ACADEMIC TEXTS IN DIFFERENT DISCIPLINES

In addition to these general characteristics of academic language, the academic texts in each discipline have specific features that make it difficult for ELLs and SELs to comprehend or produce them. Math textbooks are difficult to read because they contain mathematical symbols and expressions, diagrams and other figures, and natural language. In addition, many common words, such as *point*, have meanings specific to math. Math also has complex expressions, such as *least common multiple* and *negative exponent*. Further, ELLs and SELs often fail to notice the difference between expressions like *divided into* and *divided by*, but the difference is important for understanding the operation to be completed. Science also contains diagrams and other figures as well as technical vocabulary. In history texts, students are required to read primary documents that contain archaic language.

Language arts contains academic language as well. The syntax of stories is often quite different from conversational syntax. For instance, consider the sentence, "Once upon a time, in a far distant land, there lived a man who had three beautiful daughters." Conversational English would be quite different, "A man with three beautiful daughters lived in a distant land." Even stories for young students have sentences like, "Up jumped the gingerbread man, and down the road he ran." Here, *up* and *down* are moved to positions in front of the verbs, whereas in conversational language they would follow the verbs.

More advanced literature often contains long, complex sentences. For example, in *The Wings of the Dove* Henry James (1902) wrote the following sentence, "The fact bloomed for him, in the firelight and lamplight that glowed their welcome through the London fog, as the flower of her difference; just as her difference itself—part of which was her striking him as older in a degree for which no mere couple of months could account—was the fruit of their intimate relation" (p. 340). Although his sentences are extremely long and complex, literature contains many examples of sentences like these, and students need to learn to read literature with this complex syntax. In addition, the technical vocabulary used to analyze literature, such as *hyperbole*, *setting*, and *plot* do not appear in literature, so students cannot acquire this vocabulary by simply reading literary texts.

As these examples show, whereas academic texts in general may be characterized as containing technical vocabulary and being lexically dense and abstract, each academic discipline has its own features that make understanding oral presentations and reading and writing texts difficult for SELs and ELLs. When teachers teach both academic language and academic content, ELLs and SELs have more chances to succeed. Often teachers do teach the technical vocabulary of their disciplines, but it is also necessary to teach academic grammar and syntax.

REFLECT AND APPLY

Look over a textbook that is being used in your school with your students. Choose a passage from the textbook, and analyze it as we have done for lexical density, technical vocabulary, and abstraction. What did you discover? What kinds of difficulties might your students have with the text?

CONCLUSION

As views of grammar and syntax have changed, the way teachers teach grammar and syntax have also changed. There was a shift from a heavy emphasis on traditional grammar teaching for ELLs and SELs to little or no teaching of grammar or syntax. Currently, there is a move back to having teachers write language objectives and to teach grammar with an emphasis on the grammar of academic language.

CHAPTER THREE

Practical Application to the Classroom for Grammar and Syntax

TEACHING GRAMMAR IN CONTEXT

Teachers who teach grammar in the context of students' writing and speech (Weaver, 1996) build on the tradition of the early studies in rhetoric. When instruction applies directly to student writing, it helps them produce more effective pieces. Students need many opportunities for meaningful writing, and when they have produced a good piece of writing, they are motivated to edit it to ensure that the grammar and syntax are conventional. Students can also be shown how to enhance the rhetorical effects of their writing through careful organization and choice of examples.

Using Sentence Frames

An example from an elementary class shows how a teacher helped her students write complex sentences. The fourth-grade ELLs and SELs were writing simple sentences or compound sentences connected by "and." The teacher wanted them to begin to write complex sentences. One strategy she used was sentence frames. The class had just finished reading *Mañana Iguana* (Long, 2004), a story based on the familiar little red hen folktale. The teacher chose this version because her students lived in a rural area in the Southwest where iguanas were common. The teacher divided her students into groups. Each group was given a vocabulary word like *disappointed*, *frustrated*, or *exhausted*. They were also given a sentence frame, "Iguana was _____ because _____. The groups completed their sentences using their vocabulary word and then supplying a reason. One group wrote, "Iguana was frustrated because she had to do all the work." Another group wrote, "Iguana was depressed because nobody would help her." When they finished, the groups put their sentences on sentence strips and inserted them into a semantic web chart that all the students could see.

Sentence frames are a good way to scaffold students' development of more complex syntactic structures. A third-grade teacher was teaching a unit on Africa. Students chose a country to research and then developed a travel brochure to attract people to the country. The teacher gave students sentence frames for each of the paragraphs in the brochure. "You should travel to _____ because _____. Students completed this sentence by listing three reasons someone should visit their country. To help structure the remaining paragraphs, the teacher gave students sentence starters such as "First of all _____", "Another reason _____", and "Finally _____." This scaffolded instruction enabled her students to write well-structured travel brochures.

Sentence Combining

In secondary classes, teachers can introduce advanced grammar and syntactic structures for their more proficient ELLs and SELs. For example, one secondary teacher decided to teach her advanced ELLs and SELs to use participle phrases used as adjectives through a sentence combining activity. First, the teacher explained that participles are present and past tense verb forms like "ringing" and "rung," and they can be used in different ways in a sentence. One way is to modify a noun, as in "the swollen river" and "Walking slowly, the man looked at the river." She gave several other examples and then had students work in small groups to find participles in novels they were reading. When the students were able to identify participles used as adjectives, the teacher gave them a series of sentences to combine, such as the following:

The boy ran across the yard.

He tripped on a hose.

The hose was stretched across the lawn.

The boy hurt his shoulder.

The teacher told the students to combine each set of sentences into one or two complex sentences using participle phrases. The students worked in pairs to combine the sentences, and then they shared their sentences with their classmates. One pair combined the set of sentences about the boy this way: "Running across the yard, the boy tripped on a hose stretched across the lawn, hurting his shoulder." Through practice with combining sentences such as these and sharing them with classmates, the students learned how to vary their writing by incorporating participles. Later, the teacher taught students to avoid using dangling participles. She explained that an initial participle phrase must be followed by a subject. She wrote, "Running across the yard, a hose caused the boy to trip." Then she explained that "running across the yard" is a dangling participle because the subject, "the boy," has to follow the introductory phrase here. The hose is not running. The teacher gave other examples and had her students look for and correct dangling participles in their writing.

Mini Lessons—Cleft Sentences

A second way for ELLs and SELs to vary their sentences is by using a structure that is referred to as a cleft sentence. Like the sentences with participle phrases, cleft sentences can be used by students at the advanced levels, and even if they don't use them often in their own writing, they need to understand them in the texts they read, so teaching students about cleft sentences is useful.

In a lesson on using cleft sentences, the teacher explained that they usually start with "What" or "It" and then the subject is moved to the right of the verb. He showed the students that instead of writing, "I hoped that the results of the experiment would confirm my hypothesis," he could transform the sentence and write, "What I hoped was that the results of the experiment would confirm my hypothesis." He gave several other examples and then gave the students a series of sentences to transform by starting each sentence with "What."

Next, the teacher gave examples of cleft sentences beginning with "It.' He gave the example: "Claudius murdered the king." he showed that this sentence could be rewritten as, "It was Claudius who murdered the king." Again, the teacher had students work together to transform a series of sentences by starting with "It."

Next, the teacher showed his students that both of these kinds of cleft sentences appear in negative form. He gave them examples, such as, "I hoped the experiment would confirm my hypothesis. What I did not hope for was that the experiment would disprove the hypothesis" or "Claudius murdered the king. It was not Hamlet who murdered the king."

After providing several examples, the teacher gave his students several positive sentences and asked them to write the negative using a cleft following the model, "He knew the names of the states. What he didn't know was the names of the capitals of each state." And "He knew the names of the states. It was the names of the capitals that he didn't know." The lessons on participles and cleft sentences provide students with advanced grammatical structures that occur in academic writing. Students with higher levels of English proficiency can learn to read and write these structures.

Using Passives Effectively

Teachers generally encourage students to write using active voice. Active voice is appropriate for writing narratives and reports. However, sin some cases, passive sentences are more effective. Passive voice is often used in science and history when the focus is on what was done rather than on who did it. For example, in writing a procedural recount, the student does not have to write, "First we collected seeds. Then we classified the seeds. We sorted them into five categories." The use of active voice here puts the focus on the people doing the experiment. However, the focus should be on the steps the students followed.

By using passives, students can shift the focus. For example, they could write, "First seeds were collected. Then they were classified. They were sorted into five categories." Of course, the writer could also combine these three sentences into one passive sentence.

Once students understand the purpose of passive voice, a teacher can carry out different lessons to help students learn to write in passive voice. One tenth-grade teacher began with a mini lesson. She wrote a simple sentence on the board: "The dog chased the cat." Then she asked students who was doing the action in this sentence, and the students all chose the dog. Next, she asked who was being acted on, and students responded, "The cat." The teacher explained that the actor in this sentence is the subject and the one being acted on is the object. She labeled "the dog" as the subject and "the cat" as the object.

As a next step, the teacher asked, "How could we change the sentence to make the cat the subject but still keep the same meaning?" Students talked together and then suggested the sentence, "The cat was chased by the dog." The teacher explained that this structure was a passive sentence. She worked with the students to show the steps involved in transforming an active sentence into a passive sentence. Then she gave students a passage from their history textbook and asked them to identify passive sentences in the passage. The students practiced identifying passive sentences in different texts.

When students could easily identify most passive sentences in a passage, the teacher had students rewrite the sentences into active voice. The class discussed whether active or passive sentences were more effective. As a final step, the teacher gave the students passages and had them change the active sentences into passive sentences. Throughout the series of lessons, the class discussed when to use passives and when active sentences were more effective.

Lessons that focus on specific grammatical structures that students read and write can help them develop the grammar of academic language. Sentence, paragraph, or whole text frames can help ELLs and SELs structure their writing. More advanced students can benefit from lessons on sentence combining and mini lessons on grammatical structures such as participle phrases, cleft sentences, and effective use of passives. Lessons on specific grammatical structures followed by practice and independent use help build the academic language proficiency ELLs and SELs need to succeed in school.

REFLECT AND APPLY

We provided some examples of how teachers used sentence, paragraph, and whole text frames to help students make their writing more academic. We also showed how teachers could teach sentence combining and use a series of mini lessons to teach more advanced structures, such as participle phrases, cleft sentences, and passives. Consider a structure that you would like your students to be able to use in their writing, and teach it to your students using a frame structure or mini lessons. Be prepared to share the lesson and the results.

Lessons Based on Structural Functional Linguistics

The work of Halliday (1994) and other structural functional linguists has led to the development of curriculum based on the view of grammar as a functional resource. This approach involves teaching academic genres. Genres are types of texts, such as explanations, descriptions, and procedures. Teachers following this approach teach students the structure of the different academic genres and the language used in the genres.

A Lesson on Magnets

Gibbons (2009, 2014) gives many examples of how teachers can develop curriculum based on the view of language as functional resource. She shows how successful teachers scaffold instruction to help second language learners develop the genres they need to communicate successfully in classroom settings.

For example, she describes how a teacher scaffolds language in a lesson on magnets. Fourth-grade students work in small groups to discover how magnets attract or repel certain objects. Then the teacher demonstrates how magnets work and uses and defines the terms *attract* and *repel*. Then she scaffolds students' language as they make oral reports of their findings from the small group activity and helps them use terms like *attract* and *repel*. Finally, students write about the experiments in their science notebooks.

The teacher might extend the lesson by showing students a model report on a science topic, deconstructing the report working with the students, and then constructing a new report on another science topic following the model. Once students learn to write science reports, they could use the notes from their science notebooks to write a report on magnets following the report genre.

This sequence of having students do a science activity in small groups, giving a short demonstration lesson to introduce key concepts, scaffolding students' oral reports, and then having students write builds their academic language and their academic content knowledge. Gibbons's approach is based on the idea of language as a functional resource that develops in contexts of use. That is, as students use language for real purposes, such as reporting on their group work and writing the results of their experiments, they build the language they need to communicate effectively in academic contexts.

Text Level Deconstruct and Reconstruct

An important component of the Teaching and Learning Cycle based on a view of language as a functional resource is the deconstruction and reconstruction of a model text. One high school biology teacher wanted his students to write the steps they took to dissect a frog. They had carried out the procedure, and now they were ready to write a procedural recount. A recount is a retelling of an experience.

The teacher began by bringing in an example of a procedural recount a student from another class had written to tell about an experiment he had conducted. The teacher projected the report and read through it with his class. Then he discussed with the students how the recount was organized. It had a title, an introduction that briefly gave an overview of the procedure, and then a series of paragraphs to describe the steps. At the end was a short summary conclusion.

When the students were familiar with the components of the genre, the teacher had them look at how the paragraphs were connected. The students recognized that the writer had used time sequence words, such as *first*, *then*, and *finally*. They also noticed that the writer used past tense verbs.

After the class had worked to deconstruct this model text, the teacher worked with them to construct a recount using the information from their frog dissection activity. He reminded the students of the parts of a procedural recount and the importance of connecting sentences with time sequence words and using past tense verbs. Later, students wrote their own recounts of procedures with a focus on using signal words and past tense verb forms.

Read and Retell

Read and Retell (Brown & Cambourne, 1987) is a strategy that is consistent with Gibbons's approach. The authors have developed an effective way for students to improve in reading and writing different genres. This is a procedure they call "Read and Retell." Students read extensively in one genre, such as social studies reports. Each day, the teacher selects a short example of the genre the students have been reading. He writes the title on the board. Then he tells the students to write one or two sentences about what a report with such a title might include. After they have written their predictions, he asks them to write down some words or phrases they might find in this report if their prediction from the title is right.

Next, students form groups of three or four. They take turns reading their predictions to the group. Then, each student makes a comment on the written predictions of one other member of the group. Everyone else listens. At this point, the teacher passes out the excerpt, usually no more than a page, and everyone reads the text. The teacher may read it aloud first and then have the students read it over to themselves. Or the teacher may simply ask the students to read silently, depending on their level of English proficiency. After this, students are asked to do a written retelling. They turn over the paper with the excerpt, and write their retelling on the back without looking at the excerpt. They work quickly and don't worry about neatness or spelling. When students have had time to write their retellings, they find a partner and compare their retelling with their partner's retelling.

They ask each other questions, such as, "What did I include or omit that is different from what you included or omitted? Why did you omit a certain part? Are there any parts that I got mixed up? Does it change the meaning of the excerpt in a significant way? Did you paraphrase effectively? If you could take part of my retelling and put it in yours, what would you borrow?"

Brown and Cambourne (1987) report that repeated use of the Read and Retell strategy improves students' reading and writing.

They found that many of the words, phrases, and structures students used in their written retellings appeared later in the students' other written work. This process of focused reading and writing helps students gain greater understanding of the different academic genres.

REFLECT AND APPLY

Look over the lessons on teaching academic grammar and syntax described in this chapter. With your students, try one of these, and be prepared to report back the results.

CHAPTER FOUR

Fostering Literacy With Grammar and Syntax

READING AND WRITING ACADEMIC TEXTS

Both ELL and SEL students need to read and write academic texts. Teachers can help students develop academic literacy by teaching the grammar and syntax of academic language. All too often, the focus of instruction is on vocabulary, but as we discussed in Chapter 2, academic texts pose challenges beyond the word level. In this chapter we discuss how teachers can support ELLs and SELs by teaching the grammar and syntax of academic texts.

TEACHING GRAMMAR AND SYNTAX AT DIFFERENT LEVELS

To help ELLs and SELs develop academic language proficiency, teachers can teach grammar and syntax by focusing on different levels starting with the text level and then moving to the paragraph and sentence levels.

TEXT-LEVEL GRAMMAR AND SYNTAX

The first thing students need to communicate effectively in academic settings is to understand the different genres of each subject area. An academic genre is a type of text that is commonly used in an academic discipline. In language arts, some typical genres are plays, poetry, and narratives. In social studies typical genres would be historical recounts and accounts. In science students read and write procedures and explanations. Word problems in math are a genre as well. Each genre is structured in a particular way, and effective communication requires students to follow the expected patterns of the genre. Research by systemic functional linguists (Schleppegrell 2004) has helped educators understand genres and how to teach them.

Various academic genres are structured differently. For example, one genre students need to read and write is a historical recount. This genre recounts a historical event. Historical recounts typically include a section giving background by summarizing previous events leading up to the event that will be described. This is followed by a description of the events as they occurred. Historical recounts end with a section in which the writer or speaker explains the significance of the events.

Other genres have different components. For example, reports have a title followed by a general statement that identifies the topic and explains its relationship to other topics. A report on pine trees would identify them as a certain type of tree. The general statement usually includes the subtopics of the report. Then there is information on each of the subtopics. Finally, there may be a summarizing comment.

Structures and Features of Genres

Genres have both predictable structures and predictable grammatical features. For example, a procedure would include imperative verb forms, and a procedural recount would use past tense verbs. A personal recount would have first-person pronouns, and a historical recount would use third person. Recounts would use time sequence conjunctions, while accounts and explanations would use cause-and-effect connectors. For ELLs and SELs, the challenge is to understand the general components of each genre and then use the grammatical forms common to the genre. When teachers of the different academic subjects model and carefully teach the different genres their students are expected to read and write, they provide the scaffolded instruction students need to develop the academic language.

Teaching Academic Genres

In her book *Engaging Students in Academic Literacies: Genre-Based Pedagogy for K–5 Classrooms*, Brisk (2015) provides a detailed account of how she worked with preservice and in-service teachers in two urban schools with many ELLs and SELs over a period of 5 years using the curriculum cycle. During this time, she helped them develop a genre-based pedagogy that involved students in reading and writing different academic genres.

Through intensive summer sessions, monthly professional development, and weekly in-classroom support, Brisk, her colleagues, and graduate students worked with teachers at these two schools to transform their writing instruction. After the first year, teachers met together and planned their writing curriculum. The teachers used a curriculum cycle that was expanded to meet the needs of English learners. For example, the teachers provided a graphic organizer to aid students in understanding the structure of each genre. For English learners at lower levels of proficiency, their finished work could be a graphic that they created rather than a full piece of writing.

Brisk describes in detail how teachers taught different genre units and how they were adapted to different grade levels. For example, in the procedures unit in Grade 1, teachers and students jointly constructed a text for a procedure students had seen demonstrated. The students used prepared sentence strips to present the procedure and then added images to the steps. In Grade 5 students wrote the procedures needed to set up simple science experiments but did not use sentence strips or images.

For each genre, Brisk (2015) lists "suggestions for unit preparation and teaching of purpose, stages of the genre (text structure), and aspects of language that would be most helpful to develop in order for children to write in that particular genre" (p. x). The genres include procedures, recounts, reports, explanations, arguments, and fictional narratives. Brisk's book explains how the curriculum cycle, also referred to as the Teaching and Learning Cycle, can be used in classrooms to teach all students, including emergent bilinguals, to write the academic genres.

REFLECT AND APPLY

Choose a subject area, and a type of genre within that subject area. For example, you might choose to have students write a historical account of an important event in history. Have students look at some newspaper accounts of recent events. Once students understand the information an account needs, work with students to analyze an example of a historical account. Then work together with students to write an account. Finally, have students work independently to write a historical account. You could also follow this procedure with a different genre. With the added scaffolding you provided, were students able to write clear historical accounts? Be prepared to share your lesson and the results.

PARAGRAPH-LEVEL GRAMMAR AND SYNTAX

Often, ELLs and SELs have difficulty in writing paragraphs that follow the conventions of academic writing. Writing that is judged to be good academic writing contains different features that give it cohesion. Schleppegrell (2004) points out that writers connect ideas by using pronouns, conjunctions, and nominalization, among other strategies. Consider the following paragraph:

> The soldiers and priests of New Spain were already acquainted with raising cattle in Spain. Many were skilled horsemen. Even so, they needed help in rounding up the livestock on their sprawling lands.

We have underlined the subject of each sentence in the paragraph. The subject of the first sentence is "The soldiers and priests of New Spain." The next sentence starts with the pronoun, "Many," which refers to the soldiers and priests. The subject of the third sentence is "they," another pronoun that refers to the soldiers and priests. The subject of each sentence is linked to the subjects of the other sentences, and the result is a cohesive paragraph.

Writers also use conjunctions, such as *however*, *nevertheless*, and *as a result*, to connect sentences and give texts cohesion. Often ELLs and SELs know only a limited number of these conjunctions. They may use a word like *because* every time they try to show cause and effect. Students need to develop a greater repertoire of conjunctions and begin to use more academic words and phrases, such as *consequently* or *for that reason.*

A third device writers use to connect sentences is nominalization. Earlier, we explained that nominalization is a process of turning verbs or adjectives into nouns. For example, the verb *procrastinate* can become the noun *procrastination* by the addition of the suffix *–ion.* The adjective *sincere* becomes the noun *sincerity* with the addition of *–ity.* Sentences in academic writing are often connected by the process of nominalization. The paragraph about the soldiers and priests of New Spain relies primarily on pronouns for cohesion. If the next sentence read, "This need was filled by Native Americans" the nominal form *need* would link with the verb *need* in the previous sentence and provide more cohesion.

Teachers can teach these cohesive devices to help students improve their paragraphs. Elementary teachers, for example, could teach students to check that each pronoun they use refers to a noun that occurred earlier. Students might draw an arrow from each pronoun to its antecedent. Teachers could also ask students to check to be sure that the pronoun and the antecedent agree in number and gender. Secondary students could practice using more advanced forms, such as nominals, to connect sentences. In addition, they could practice adding signal words and phrases, such as *in the same way* or *nevertheless* to connect sentences in their paragraphs and to connect one paragraph to the next.

REFLECT AND APPLY

Find a passage from a textbook your students are reading that has clear connections among the sentences. Ask students to work together to circle pronouns, conjunctions, and nominalizations that give the paragraph cohesion. Report back on how the lesson went.

THREE TYPES OF PARAGRAPH COHESION

Brown (2009) describes three ways that writers create cohesive paragraphs. He begins by explaining that sentences can be divided into two parts: the topic and the comment. The topic is the beginning of the sentence or clause, and the comment is what follows. The comment "is the place where the writer develops the message of the sentence or clause, where the writer 'comments on' the Topic" (p. 72). These two sections correspond to the subject and predicate of the sentence. For example, in the first sentence from the example in the previous paragraph, "The soldiers and priests of New Spain were already acquainted with raising cattle in Spain," the topic is 'The soldiers and priests of New Spain" and the comment is the remainder of the sentence. Writers can link sentences in a paragraph by connecting the topic of one sentence with either the topic or the comment of the preceding sentence. Brown refers to the ways of connecting sentences in a paragraph as constant, derived, or chained. Writers may use just one of these patterns or, more commonly, combine all three.

Constant Topic

The paragraph about the soldiers and priests provides a good example of the first pattern: a constant topic. The topics are "The soldiers and priests of New Spain," "Many," "they." The topic of each sentence is the soldiers and priests. The writing is varied through the use of the pronouns, *many* and *they*, but the topic is constant. By keeping a constant topic, a writer creates cohesion. Many students produce paragraphs in which the sentences do not seem to connect to one another. A good first step might be to teach them this constant topic pattern and have them practice using the pattern in their writing.

Derived Topic

A second pattern that Brown (2009) identifies is a derived topic. This pattern is similar to the constant topic. However, instead of all the topics being the same, the topic of the first sentence is more general, and the topics of the following sentences are derived from or examples of the first topic. For example, if the topic of the first sentence is plants, a derived topic might be a type of plant, such as a dandelion. The following paragraph illustrates this pattern:

<u>Different immigrant groups</u> settled the West. <u>Eastern city dwellers</u> came for the promise of new land. <u>Unemployed workers</u> came to find work in the new territories. <u>Adventurers</u> came to seek gold.

As this example shows, paragraphs that follow the derived pattern are often used when writers give examples of a general topic. Here, the first sentence introduces the general topic, immigrant groups, and the following sentences each describe one type of group. The result is a cohesive paragraph.

Chained Topic

The third pattern Brown discusses is chaining. Chaining occurs when the comment of one sentence becomes the topic of the next sentence. The following paragraph contains sentences that are chained:

The discovery of gold in California led to an influx of <u>fortune seekers</u>. <u>Many of these men and women</u> landed in <u>San Francisco</u>. <u>The city</u> grew very rapidly with this influx of <u>new residents</u>. <u>Not all of the people</u> who came were honest.

The comment in the first sentence ends with "fortune seekers." The next sentence begins with "Many of these men and women," a reference to the fortune seekers. The second sentence ends with 'San Francisco," and the following sentence begins with 'the city." This paragraph is cohesive because the topic of each sentence connects with the comment of the previous sentence. Chaining is the most common way that writers of academic texts create cohesion, but most academic texts use all three patterns.

Teaching Paragraph Cohesion

Brown suggests several activities to help students learn how to use the three patterns to give their paragraphs greater cohesion. First, the teacher explains what the topic of a clause is and has students practice finding the topics of a series of sentences. Then the teacher explains that the rest of a clause is called the comment. Students divide clauses into the topic and comment.

Once students can identify the topic and comment of clauses, the teacher introduces the three patterns for paragraph cohesion one at a time. Students are given paragraphs for each type of cohesion and asked to find the connections between sentences. They can also identify places where there are no links between sentences as well. Once they have identified these places, they can write or rewrite a sentence to create a link. After students are able to write paragraphs with a constant topic, the teacher can continue by teaching them how to connect sentences with derived and chained topics.

To write in the academic genres, ELLs and SELs need to write cohesive paragraphs. Teachers can help students write cohesive paragraphs by explaining the three ways to connect sentences and then having students practice writing and rewriting paragraphs to make them more cohesive.

REFLECT AND APPLY

Choose a subject area (science, language arts, or social studies) and a topic (photosynthesis, theme of a novel, or indigenous groups in the Midwest). Then write three paragraphs on the topic you chose using different types of paragraph cohesion. One paragraph should have a constant topic, the next a derived topic, and the last a chained topic. Share the paragraphs with your colleagues. What did you notice about writing these three paragraphs? Do you think it would be helpful to use this approach to teaching paragraph cohesion with your students?

SENTENCE-LEVEL GRAMMAR AND SYNTAX

Complex sentences are typical of academic language, and ELLs and SELs are expected to be able to read and write texts that contain complex sentences. Here is a short passage typical of what is written in history texts:

Washington's troops struggled to defeat the British because they lacked supplies and organization. Since many of the men who volunteered were farmers and tradesmen with no military training and no long-term commitment to fighting in a war that they didn't fully understand, Washington had difficulty planning his campaign.

These two sentences contain six clauses. Readers need to figure out how the ideas in these clauses are related to one another and which are the main ideas. This is a formidable challenge for ELLs and SELs. Teachers can help students with reading and writing texts with multiple clauses by showing them the different ways clauses are combined in English. While traditional approaches to teaching grammar are not effective for improving students' reading or writing, a close examination of the language in students' textbooks or in their own writing using a systemic functional approach can give students insights into how sentences are structured.

TYPES OF CLAUSES

In traditional grammar, clauses are categorized as independent or dependent. Independent clauses can stand alone as complete sentences, but dependent clauses must be connected to an independent clause. In the first sentence of the history passage, for example, the first clause, "Washington's troops struggled to defeat the British," is independent because it could stand as a complete sentence by itself. The second clause, "because they lacked supplies and organization," is dependent since it is not a complete sentence. The second sentence begins with a dependent clause that is followed by an independent clause. Students must recognize that the main ideas are in independent clauses, and the dependent clauses provide additional information about the independent clause. In these sentences, the dependent clauses provide reasons for the facts in the independent clauses.

Functional linguists distinguish between two types of dependent clauses. Some dependent clauses are connected to the independent clause by a conjunction such as *because*. In the passage about the troops, the second clause is of this type. Some dependent clauses are embedded within another clause. In the second sentence, the clauses, "who volunteered" and "that they didn't fully understand" are embedded inside the dependent clause.

A common function of an embedded clause is to provide more information about a noun that precedes it. In the previous example, the embedded clauses tell the reader more about the men in the army and the war. Embedding clauses results in long noun phrases: "men who volunteered" and "a war that they didn't fully understand." Such complex nominal phrases are typical of academic writing, and teachers should discuss how embedded clauses function in academic writing so that ELLs and SELs can better understand what they read and also begin to write sentences with embedded clauses.

SENTENCE-LEVEL DECONSTRUCT AND RECONSTRUCT

One way that teachers can help students understand the complex writing of academic texts is through a process Fang (2008) refers to as Deconstruct Reconstruct. For example, the teacher might begin with a short passage like the one about Washington's army. The teacher should choose a passage that is important for students to understand because the goal is always to teach both language and content.

> Washington's troops struggled to defeat the British because they lacked supplies and organization. Since many of the men who volunteered were farmers and tradesmen with no military training and no long-term commitment to fighting in a war that they didn't fully understand, Washington had difficulty planning his campaign.

The teacher works with the students to rewrite the passage into a series of simple sentences. In this paragraph one of the clauses has a compound object of the preposition, and it contains two important ideas, so the teacher rewrites the two noun phrases as separate simple sentences. This produces the following:

> Washington's troops struggled to defeat the British
>
> They lacked supplies and organization.
>
> Many of the men were farmers and tradesmen with no military training.
>
> They had no long-term commitment to fighting in a war
>
> The men volunteered
>
> They didn't fully understand the war
>
> Washington had difficulty planning his campaign.

Next, the teacher passes the list of sentences out to the students. Then the students, working in groups, decide how to combine the simple sentences into complex sentences without looking at the original passage. When they finish, the groups write or project their results on the board and explain the process they went through as they decided how to combine the sentences. The class then creates a composite paragraph using ideas from all the groups. What is important here is for students to talk about how and why they combined sentences as they did. Students can also compare their reconstructed paragraphs with the original. In some cases, students may decide they like their version better than what the published author wrote.

Combining Sentences

To scaffold this activity, the teacher can give students practice in combining sentences beginning with non-embedded clauses. The teacher should use examples related to the content the class is studying. The teacher might begin with two simple sentences logically related by cause and effect, such as "Washington's troops struggled to defeat the British. They lacked supplies and organization," and discuss different ways they could be combined. Students might write, "Washington's troops struggled to defeat the British since they lacked supplies and organization." They could discuss the difference between this sentence and one that begins with the clause about supplies and organization: "They lacked supplies and organization; therefore, Washington's troops struggled to defeat the British." This process helps the students understand that the order of clauses can be changed. The class can also discuss the idea that the clause that comes first is the one the writer wants the reader to focus on. One order puts the focus on Washington's troops' struggle, and the other emphasizes the lack of organization and supplies. After students have practiced with other pairs of sentences showing cause and effect, the teacher can introduce sentences related in other ways, such as sequence.

When students understand how to combine sentences using non-embedded clauses, the teacher can introduce embedded clauses. The teacher might give students two sentences such as "Washington's troops struggled to defeat the British" and "They were disorganized and lacked supplies." First, students can discuss how these two sentences can be combined to show cause and effect. Then, the teacher can show them that the sentences can also be combined by putting one clause inside the other to produce "Washington's troops, who lacked organization and supplies, struggled to defeat the British." Then, students can practice this new way of combining clauses with other sentence pairs.

After showing students the two basic ways of combining clauses, teachers can have students analyze passages in their textbooks to see how the writers combined ideas into complex sentences. Students can also begin to use these kinds of sentences in their own writing. Carefully scaffolded instruction on the structure of complex sentences can help ELLs and struggling readers and writers understand and produce academic texts.

REFLECT AND APPLY

Choose an important passage from a textbook the students are reading, a passage that has information you want your students to remember. Do the Deconstruct Reconstruct activity using the passage. Be prepared to share your lesson and the results with your colleagues.

SIGNAL WORDS

As students learn to combine simple sentences in different ways to produce more complex writing, they need to develop a repertoire of words and phrases to connect clauses. Many ELLs and SELs overuse a few common connectors because their vocabulary is limited. One way to help students move past this early stage is to build their vocabulary by introducing other, more precise, words to show the relationships between ideas. These transition words are often referred to as signal words because they signal to the reader how two ideas are related. Signal words may connect ideas within a sentence or across sentences. Fisher, Rothenberg, and Frey (2007) explain how a team of ninth-grade teachers worked to help their students develop signal words to link ideas.

The teachers examined student writing and found that their ELLs and SELs often left transitions out. The teachers found a word list that grouped signal words by function. The functions included addition, example, comparison, contrast, cause and effect, concession, and conclusion. For each function, they listed several words. For example, for *addition*, the list included *also, and, besides, furthermore, in addition, indeed, in fact, moreover, so,* and *too* (Fisher et al., 2007, p. 52).

The teachers posted a list with one or two signal words for each function in their rooms as a word wall. They took time on a regular basis to review the words with their students. As they read aloud to their students, they made a point of emphasizing words in the texts that were on the list. Students also added new words for each function. According to Fisher and his colleagues, "Over time, students started to notice the terms in their reading and began incorporating them into their writing" (p. 51). The process the teachers used enabled the struggling SELs and ELLs in their ninth-grade classes to enrich their academic vocabulary by adding signal words and phrases that showed logical connections between ideas.

REFLECT AND APPLY

Signal words have different functions. Post the following functions with some signal word examples in your classroom. Add more signal words for each function during your teaching as they come up in readings and discussion. Be prepared to share the function words that come up in your class.

Addition: also, furthermore

Example: for example, such as

Cause and effect: because, therefore

Sequence: first, next, last

Comparison: similarly, in a like manner

Contrast: but, on the other hand

Concession: nevertheless, however

Conclusion: finally, in sum

ADDITIONAL ACTIVITIES
TO DEVELOP ACADEMIC SYNTAX

Fang (2008) describes another strategy to help ELLs and SELs read and write complex academic sentences. This strategy involves translating or paraphrasing an informational text written in academic language into everyday spoken English. For this strategy, students work in small groups to develop a radio show series they will record on tape. The teacher gives each group a short informational text. The groups rewrite the text into a 3- to 5-minute segment for a radio talk show. Once students write the text, they practice reading it on audiotape. They listen to the recording and compare it with the original informational text. They can also discuss the kinds of changes they made to convert the written text into speech. This is a good activity for ELLs and SELs because it helps them understand the differences between spoken and written language.

Using Predictable Books

Younger ELLs and SELs as well as older ELLs and SELs at beginning levels of English literacy proficiency can develop their knowledge of syntax by reading and writing predictable books. Many books for beginning readers follow a predictable pattern. For example, *Mom* (Randell, Giles, & Smith, 1996) follows a consistent pattern. On page one, the text reads, "Mom is cooking" (p. 2). Each of the following pages shows a picture of Mom doing a different activity, and the text on each page follows the same pattern. Pages include "Mom is painting" (p. 4), "Mom is swimming" (p. 8), and "Mom is reading" (p. 14). This book is predictable because only the verb changes and the syntactic pattern is constant. By reading books such as these, ELLs and SELs receive repeated exposure to the pattern. They can follow up by writing their own books about family members using this pattern.

Books for more advanced students can be used to introduce more complex syntactic patterns. For example, in the book *I Love You More* (Duksta, 2007), the mother compares her love for her child using comparatives in complex structures, including "I love you higher than the highest bird ever flew" (p. 3). Each page contains another comparison using the same syntactic structure. ELLs and SELs hearing or reading this book will acquire this syntactic structure over time, and then they can write their own books using this pattern.

REFLECT AND APPLY

Look for some predictable limited-text books that would be appropriate for your ELL or SEL students. Bring the books to share with your colleagues. If you teach older students, be sure the content and pictures are age appropriate.

Using Cloze Passages

Another strategy for teaching syntax is to use Cloze passages. Typically Cloze passages are created by deleting words following a pattern such as every fifth word. However, Cloze passages can also be developed by deleting targeted words or phrases. For example, a teacher could delete the auxiliary verbs in a passage, and students would need to supply the correct verb forms. Or a teacher could delete comparatives in a passage for students to fill in. Selective Cloze activities can be written to give students practice with different syntactic structures.

For example, the following paragraph could be given to students:

María **is** studying history. She **has** read about the Westward migration. She **will** write a report on this historical period. The report **will** be about 15 pages long. María hopes she **can** complete this assignment successfully.

The auxiliary verbs, which we have put in bold here, could be deleted to create a Cloze passage. Students could work in pairs to fill in the blanks. During this process, they should discuss their choices with one another. Then each pair can provide a word as the whole class reconstructs the passage.

REFLECT AND APPLY

Consider some grammatical structure that your students find difficult. Find or write a passage that uses that structure. Convert the passage using Cloze so that students can complete the Cloze and use the structure. Bring the passage and the results to share.

CONCLUSION

ELLs and SELs who struggle with reading and writing academic texts need to develop academic language proficiency at the text, paragraph, and sentence levels. In academic writing, genres have certain expected components or sections, and students need to understand both the structure and language typical of each genre. ELLs and SELs often have trouble writing cohesive paragraphs. Paragraphs are made cohesive by using pronouns, conjunctions, and nominalizations. Brown (2009) outlines three patterns that connect sentences within a paragraph. Teachers can help students write more cohesive paragraphs by explicitly teaching them how to connect their sentences.

Teachers can also work with students to help them develop an academic style of writing at the sentence level. Sentences in academic writing are generally complex and consist of several clauses. Students need to understand the complex structure of academic sentences to write and read academic texts. Teachers can help students develop academic syntax by having them deconstruct and reconstruct key passages, read and write predictable books, and complete Cloze passages.

CHAPTER FIVE

Assessing Grammar and Syntax

ELLs and SELs generally score low on state and national summative tests. This has become even more evident when reviewing the results of tests designed to assess the Common Core standards. It is not surprising that ELLs and SELs score low on these tests as research has consistently shown that it takes from 5 to 7 or more years for these students to develop academic language proficiency at a level equivalent to native speakers of standard English. Summative test results may discourage both students and teachers. In addition, these tests do not provide information teachers can use to guide their teaching.

USING FORMATIVE ASSESSMENT

In contrast, formative assessments can help teachers with curriculum decisions. These tests are designed to help teachers determine students' current abilities to plan the next steps in instruction. MacDonald and her colleagues (2015) state that formative assessment "occurs in the midst of instruction and compares students' ongoing progress to possible trajectories of learning. It can help identify the most productive next steps in instruction" (p. xi). Formative assessment is one component of an overall assessment system that also includes interim and summative assessments. Teachers can help ELLs and SELs improve their grammar and syntax by using formative assessments to guide day-to-day instruction. With well-planned instruction, over time ELLs and SELs will develop the knowledge and skills they need to show progress on interim and summative assessments.

REFLECT AND APPLY

What have been your experiences with summative assessments? Do you or your students find the summative assessments useful? Why? Or why not?

A FOUR-STEP PROCESS
FOR USING FORMATIVE ASSESSMENT

MacDonald and her coauthors (2015) describe a four-step process teachers of ELLs and SELs can use to integrate formative assessment into teaching. The first step is to design and teach lessons that have a consistent focus on developing both academic content knowledge and academic language. To accomplish this, teachers write content objectives and then write language objectives based on the content. These language objectives provide language learning targets for the students. The second step is to sample students' language. This requires that teachers plan lessons during which students will produce language in oral or written form that can be collected. In the third step teachers analyze student language samples. They use different tools to conduct their analyses and use this information to plan further instruction. The final step is to provide formative feedback. As MacDonald and her colleagues comment, formative feedback is designed to

> give students clear, progress-oriented, and actionable information about their language use—both what they're doing well and what they can do to become more effective users of English— and to adjust instruction to meet students' needs. (p. xix)

The four steps form a cycle. The teacher plans instruction, gathers language samples, analyzes the samples, and provides formative feedback. The feedback is designed to affirm students' achievements and then outline clear next steps that students can attain.

MacDonald and her colleagues (2015) suggest that teachers analyze four elements and planning feedback: (1) genre components,

(2) text structure, (3) grammatical forms, and (4) vocabulary usage. In analyzing a writing sample or an oral report, a teacher should consider each of these components. However, when providing feedback a teacher would normally choose only one or two of them for a student to work on.

REFLECT AND APPLY

Do you use formative assessment in your classroom? How is your approach the same as or different from what MacDonald and her colleagues (2015) suggest?

LANGUAGE OBJECTIVES

Teachers of ELLs and SELs write language objectives to teach different aspects of academic language. Language objectives should be based on content objectives. For example, when teaching about the water cycle, a teacher might have students write an explanation of the cycle using signal words showing sequence to connect each stage in the cycle. The teacher's language objective could be that students would write an explanation with all the expected components. Or the teacher could choose to make the language objective that students should use correct verb forms for an explanation. A third possibility would be that students would use signal words showing sequence to connect the stages of the cycle.

The teacher can assess the language objective he or she chooses by looking at the students' writing. Depending on the language objective, the teacher could focus on whether or not the students included the expected components of an explanation, the students' use of the appropriate verb tense for an explanation, or the students' use of signal words. The key is to align the assessment with the language objective and provide feedback to help students improve their academic writing of explanations.

GENRE COMPONENTS

As we discussed earlier, genres are specific types of texts, such as procedures, reports, recounts, and analyses. These genres vary by academic subject area. A literature report is different from a history or science report. Genres are made up of several components. These components are the sections conventionally included in the genre by writers in each discipline. Knowing the components of a genre helps students in reading and writing academic texts.

For example, personal recounts that students write in language arts classes retell a series of events based on personal experience. The components of a personal recount include an orientation telling who was involved and when and where the events occurred. This section is followed by the description of a series of events organized chronologically. Personal recounts often end with an evaluative comment. In contrast, procedural recounts that students write in science classes have the goal of telling what was done to carry out an investigation. A student writing a procedural recount in science like the one we discussed in Chapter 3 would begin by explaining the aim or goal of the investigation. This would be followed by a section describing the events or steps taken in order of occurrence. A procedural recount would conclude with a report of the results or findings from the investigation (Gibbons, 2009). In analyzing student work, a teacher would look to see that all the components expected of the genre are included.

REFLECT AND APPLY

Pick out a genre that you would like your students to be able to write. Identify the components of a written piece in that genre. Post the components and provide examples of this type of genre to your students. Develop a rubric that reflects the components, and explain that this rubric will be used to evaluate their genre writing. Have them write using the genre. Ask students to read each other's writing and evaluate it with the rubric. Discuss the results with the students, and allow them to revise their writing. Use the rubric for a final evaluation of the writing. What were the results? Be prepared to share.

Text Structure

Teachers can also analyze the structure of student texts. Text structure refers to the connections between the different parts of the text. This involves checking to see whether the student used pronouns with clear referents and that all the sentences in each paragraph are connected to the main topic. In addition, the paragraphs should be linked by appropriate conjunctions. For example, in both a personal recount and a procedural recount, the paragraphs would be connected by words indicating a sequence of events, such as like *first*, *next*, and *finally*.

GRAMMATICAL STRUCTURE AND VOCABULARY

The last two elements for analysis are grammatical structure and vocabulary. Grammatical structure can refer to things like the use of complex sentences or subject-verb agreement. Vocabulary includes technical words related to the discipline as well as general academic terms such as *synthesis* and *explanation*.

Personal and procedural recounts would use past tense verbs, so teachers could look to see whether or not ELLs and SELs used correct forms, especially of irregular verbs. Each genre typically uses specific grammatical and syntactic forms. For example, while a procedural recount uses past tense verbs, a procedure uses imperative verbs. Teachers can provide formative feedback on the grammatical and syntactic structures associated with each genre as they teach it.

REFLECT AND APPLY

Using a sample passage, go over with your students how it uses connecting words, technical words, and appropriate grammar such as the correct verb tense. Have students work in pairs or groups with different passages to identify these features. Discuss with the class. Report the results.

LANGUAGE LEARNING TARGETS

To provide formative feedback that can help students improve, teachers should develop language learning targets based on the analysis of the language sample. It is important that students have a clear understanding of what they have done well and what the next steps are in making improvements. Students with similar language learning targets can be grouped together for focused instruction. ELLs and SELs can also work in pairs to provide feedback to each other.

Assessment for Kia

MacDonald and her colleagues (2015) give examples of how the four steps work with students at different proficiency levels. For example, Kia, a beginning-level ELL, wrote a report on the development of the U.S. Constitution in her sheltered social studies class. The teacher analyzed her report. She found several strengths: Kia understood some of the main ideas from her reading and included them in her report, she used three new vocabulary words, and she attempted new sentence structures.

The teacher noted that Kia did not use the expected genre components for a report, and she did not connect the sentences to one another. She tried to link clauses in a sentence using a sentence frame. She also tried to use prepositional phrases in two sentences but was not successful. The teacher met with Kia to establish language learning targets. They discussed Kia's report, and then with her teacher's help, Kia wrote down that she would write one sentence for each main idea in her assigned readings and add details using prepositional phrases. In addition, she would circle parts of her reading she didn't understand and then ask a classmate or the teacher to explain those parts. The formative feedback Kia received helped her develop language learning targets that the teacher would check for on her next paper. This specific feedback helps students like Kia develop the grammar and syntactic structures they need to read and write academic texts.

ASSESSMENT TOOLS

Teachers who use formative feedback to help English learners become more proficient in their use of academic language can use different tools to assess language for formative purposes. These tools can be used by students in evaluating their own work, by peers evaluating the work of others, or by teachers. Three useful tools are checklists, rating scales, and rubrics. Checklists contain items that students or teachers can respond to with a simple "yes" or "no." For example, using a checklist, Kia could check whether or not she included one sentence for each main idea from the reading, whether she links clauses using a sentence frame, and whether she uses propositional phrases.

Checklist for Kia

A simple checklist like this would be a useful tool to assess Kia's writing.

Kia	Yes	No
Uses one sentence for each idea	✓	
Links clauses using a sentence frame		✓
Uses prepositional phrases		✓

In a conference with the student, a teacher can quickly go over a checklist like this to provide the student with feedback and plan next steps.

Rating Scale

Another tool, a rating scale, moves beyond "yes" and "no" to indicate how well something was done. For example, Kia could judge whether what she read in her social studies book was "very clear," "somewhat clear," or "not clear." A rating scale can also indicate student performance on a continuum from "most of the time" to "not at all." Here we show a simple rating scale for Kia.

Kia	Most of the Time	Some of the Time	Not at All
What I read is clear to me.			
I write complete sentences.			
I include prepositional phrases.			

It is easy to construct rating scales like this, and they provide students with more detailed information than simple checklists.

Rubrics

Rubrics, the final tool, are more detailed and outline the criteria students should meet in various areas. For Kia a rubric could list that a good paper has one sentence for each main idea from the reading, that the ideas are linked using a sentence frame, and that some sentences include a prepositional phrase that adds details. Developing checklists, rating scales, and rubrics helps teachers make expectations clear and allows students to know exactly what they need to do to succeed.

When teachers develop rubrics for assignments and share the rubrics with students before they complete the assignment, the rubric provides a guide for the students as they work. The teacher can then use the rubric to provide formative feedback. Students can also work in pairs or small groups and assess each other's assignments using the rubric. In addition, writing the rubric helps the teacher to think through the assignment carefully and decide exactly what he or she expects the final student product to include. Here we include a rubric Kia's teacher could use to assess reports like the ones that Kia and her classmates wrote. This rubric is for students who are at intermediate or advanced levels:

	1	2	3
Genre components	Lacks a title, no statement of the components, information on only one or two subtopics, and no conclusion	Includes a title and a general statement on the topic, names one or two components, gives information on one or two subtopics, and conclusion	Includes a title, a general statement naming the components, information on each subtopic, and conclusion
Text structure	Lacks general statement that names components, has no clear subtopics, and paragraphs not connected by signal words	Some components named in general statement, one or two subtopics clearly developed, and some use of signal words to connect subtopics	Components named in general statement with each developed as a subtopic and sections connected by signal words, showing addition

	1	2	3
Grammar	Verb tense not consistent, sentences not complete, no use of prepositional phrases	Most verbs in present tense, most sentences complete, one or two sentences with prepositional phrases	Verbs written in present tense, complete sentences, some sentences with prepositional phrases
Vocabulary	Uses one or two technical words and no general academic vocabulary	Uses some technical vocabulary and some general academic vocabulary	Uses appropriate technical vocabulary taken from the reading and some general academic vocabulary

CONCLUSION

Teachers can use formative assessments to help ELLs and SELs increase their academic language proficiency. These assessments are designed to help teachers identify students' strengths and weaknesses and to determine next steps in instruction. The cycle for formative assessment begins with developing content and language objectives and then designing and teaching lessons. Next it moves to sampling student performance, analyzing the sample, and providing feedback. Teachers can use checklists, rating scales, and rubrics as tools for analysis of student work. They can also use these to have students evaluate the work of their peers. Throughout this process, teachers can involve students to ensure that they understand how they can continually improve their academic literacy.

REFLECT AND APPLY

We described different formative assessment tools including checklists, rating scales, and rubrics. Try developing each of these tools for different reading and writing assignments you give to your students. Be sure to include in the tool genre components, text structure, and grammatical structure and vocabulary. Use the tools to evaluate your students. Which tools were most helpful? Did the tools help you see how you could modify your instruction?

CHAPTER SIX

Conclusions, Challenges, and Connections

This book has focused on the grammar and syntax of academic language. Chapter 2 discussed four views of grammar. Grammar has been seen as a prescription for correct use, a functional command of sentence structure, a description of syntactic structures, and a functional resource for making meaning. Each view of grammar has led to different approaches to teaching grammar and syntax to ELLs and SELs. Chapter 2 also discussed the characteristics of academic language. Chapters 3 and 4 provided examples from elementary and secondary classes of how grammar and syntax can be taught in context to elementary and secondary students at the text, paragraph, and sentence levels. Chapter 5 outlined a four-step approach to formative assessment for grammar and syntax. Each chapter also included sections that asked readers to reflect on and apply the concepts that were discussed.

CHALLENGES FOR THE USER

The challenge for teachers is to decide when and how to teach grammar and syntax. It is important that educators across content areas address the specific components of ALD that may be their responsibility. Each teacher should look at all levels of academic language within the genres that ELLs and SELs read, write, and discuss to identify the language structures that students need.

A good approach for teachers in each content area is to focus on the specific genres their students need to read and write. For example, a science teacher might teach the structure and language of procedures and procedural recounts, and a history teacher might teach historical recounts and reports. The key is to teach both academic content and the language needed to read and write about that content.

For some readers, the challenge may be a personal one: learning more about grammar and syntax. While we do not recommend that teachers teach grammar traditionally, we do recommend that teachers understand grammar so that they can help their students work with grammar in meaningful contexts. Some readers may not have had effective grammar instruction in grade school, so they may be learning along with their own students. For these readers, it might be helpful to review the sources cited in this book. A good place to start would be Freeman and Freeman's (2014) book, *Essential Linguistics*. As with anything, the more practice and exposure to grammar and syntax we have, the better we can become at teaching those elements of ALD.

TUNING PROTOCOL: POWERFUL PROFESSIONAL LEARNING TO ENHANCE ELL AND SEL ACHIEVEMENT

To understand and implement the work of this series, we advocate sustained, job-embedded professional learning that is grounded in the work of teacher teams. Reading this book can be a starting place for such learning, and the Tuning Protocol is a tool for self-reflection when analyzing student work samples for ALD.

Specifically, the Tuning Protocol is a powerful design for professional learning that is based on collaborative analysis of student work. Due to the fact that it takes focused professional development over time to change major instructional practices, we recommend that a recursive professional development sequence, like the Tuning Protocol, be used along with the book series. The Tuning Protocol, developed by the Coalition of Essential Schools (Blythe, Allen, & Powell, 1999), can be effective as a way to more deeply explore ALD strategies and approaches recommended throughout the book series. For example, a department or grade level may choose to analyze student work samples from ELLs and/or SELs that address paragraph structures from *Grammar and Syntax in Context* or to analyze the conversational skill of clarifying ideas from *Conversational Discourse*. A full-cycle collaborative conversation of the Tuning Protocol for grammar and syntax is provided here.

THE TUNING PROTOCOL

(1) Presenter describes context of the work to be analyzed (e.g., student level, curriculum, or time allotted).

Presenter determines focus question, which will be the *lens by which the work will be analyzed*.

(2) Group silently reviews work and asks clarifying questions only (e.g., How long did it take?).

(3) Group takes notes on warm and cool feedback *regarding the focus question only*.

(4) Group shares warm and cool feedback.

(5) Presenter reflects on next steps for instruction.

(Adapted from Soto, 2012)

TUNING PROTOCOL FOR GRAMMAR AND SYNTAX

In Chapter 3, you read about using sentence frames to teach complex syntax. One of the strategies highlighted was described as follows:

> A third-grade teacher was teaching a unit on Africa. Students chose a country to research and then developed a travel brochure to attract people to the country. The teacher gave students a sentence frame for the introductory paragraph in the brochure. "You should travel to _____ because _____."
> Students completed this sentence by listing three reasons someone should visit their country. To help structure the remaining paragraphs, the teacher gave students sentence starters such as "First of all_____", "Another reason _____", and "Finally _____." This scaffolded instruction enabled her students to write well-structured travel brochures that included the components of the persuasive essay genre.

Once the teacher used the sentence frames and sentence starters to help her ELLs and SELs develop persuasive essays, the students engaged in a series of lessons designed to help them develop the vocabulary and language structures needed to complete their brochures. After the students had completed their brochures, the teacher brought a brochure completed by one of her ELLs to her department meeting for reflection. The brochure was then analyzed using the Tuning Protocol, as follows:

(1) **Teacher describes the context of the work to the group**—"I used the brochure to have students become experts on a country in Africa and assist with attracting people to the country. I used the brochure format to teach students how to write a persuasive essay. I provided my ELLs with a sentence frame for the introduction and sentence starters for each paragraph in the brochure. In this way, students could focus on the content (Africa) and were supported with linguistic structures that they will also need when they write other assignments."

   (a) **Presenter determines focus question for analysis of student sample**—The teacher decides that as her colleagues analyze the brochure, she would like them to focus on how her students could further elaborate on their descriptions of the country. The focus question then becomes: "How can I assist my ELLs with elaborating on their description of their countries?"

(2) **Group reviews work and asks clarifying questions**—One colleague asked the clarifying question: "How did you first introduce the complex sentence frames?" The teacher responds, "First, I modeled how to use the frames with a country that we read about together as a class by speaking out and then writing down my sentences under a document reader. I showed students how to take information from the reading, and include it in the frame, by highlighting and summarizing the text."

   (b) **Group individually takes notes, highlighting warm and cool feedback**—For warm feedback, participants will analyze the student work sample for everything that was done well, from punctuation to use of modal auxiliaries for persuasion. For cool (not cold) feedback, participants will analyze the student work sample according to the focus question only. Recall that the teacher presenter selected the focus question, so that she was in control of the type of cool feedback that she wished to receive. In this example, the teacher asked for the following cool feedback, "How can I assist my ELLs with elaborating on their descriptions of the countries?"

(c) **Group shares warm and cool feedback**—One at a time, participants in the group share warm feedback first. It is helpful to use objective frames when providing feedback, such as "I noticed (*for observations*)" and "I wonder (*for questions*)". It is also important to begin with warm feedback as we all want to be viewed from an asset model first. A sample warm feedback statement might be: "*I noticed* that the student included three reasons to visit Kenya." (Please note that if the Tuning Protocol is being used with a large group, the group facilitator will want to select a few warm and cool feedback statements.) Once the warm feedback has been shared, cool feedback statements can be provided. Recall that cool feedback is based on the focus question only. In this case, the teacher wanted cool feedback regarding the following question: "How can I assist my ELLs with elaborating on their reasons for visiting the country?" A sample cool feedback statement might be: "The student appeared to understand how to complete the frame by listing three reasons to visit the country, but explanation of each reason in the following paragraphs was quite brief and did not include information from research on the country. *I wonder* if providing more time and help in reading information about the country would assist this ELL with elaboration."

(3) **Presenter reflects on feedback provided**—After all of the warm and cool feedback has been provided, the teacher presenter reflects on his or her next steps from the group

discussion of the student work sample on supporting ideas. A sample reflective statement might be: "My next step with having my students, especially this ELL, elaborate on her reasons, is to provide scaffolded instruction in how to read articles to gather more information."

We recognize that for many teachers, the ideas in this book and the book series will require time and practice. Both sustained professional development over time (which can include the Tuning Protocol) and instructional coaching can be helpful tools. It is also important for educators to remember to go slow to go fast, that is, to realize that the strategies and instructional approaches outlined will take time to approximate. In this manner, just as we honor the assets of our students let's honor the assets of our teachers as excellent learners, who can take on new challenges with appropriate and sustained professional development over time.

ALD BOOK SERIES SUMMARY
AND INTERSECTIONS ACROSS BOOK SERIES

As suggested in Chapter 1, the purpose of this four-book series is to assist educators in developing expertise in, and practical strategies for, addressing the key dimensions of academic language when working with ELLs and SELs. In order to systemically address the needs of ELLs and SELs, we educators must share a common understanding of academic language development and the interconnectedness of its four dimensions.

The following chart provides a summary of the ALD dimension as well as intersections across the book series. To truly create systemic change for ELLs and SELs in the area of ALD, there must be a deep understanding of each of the dimensions of ALD under study as well as sustained professional development and instructional efforts to address each dimension, which will be addressed throughout the book series. The book series summary can assist the reader with where to begin when reading the series, and the intersections across the book series can assist with making connections as one completes each book.

This chart allows us to better understand how ALD can and will support ELLs and SELs to make connections within new, rigorous

ALD Dimension	Book Series Summary	Intersections Across Book Series
Conversational Discourse	Zwiers (2016) defines *conversational discourse* as the use of language for extended, back-and-forth, and purposeful communication among people. A key feature of conversational discourse is that it is used to create and clarify knowledge, not just transmit it. The essential skills of conversational discourse include the following: ● Conversing with a purpose ● Clarifying ideas ● Supporting ideas and finding evidence ● Evaluating evidence and reasoning ● Negotiating ideas Successful conversational discourse for ELLs and SELs requires a safe classroom culture and appropriate scaffolds for conversation.	● Conversational discourse necessarily connects to the development of *academic vocabulary* and to its written counterpart, academic writing across genres. ● It connects to *grammar and syntax in context* through the need to make and express meaning at the text, paragraph, and sentence levels. ● It connects to *culturally and linguistically responsive practices* by engaging students in cooperative practices and respectful listening to other points of view and backgrounds.
Academic Vocabulary	Calderón (2016) defines *academic vocabulary* as a combination of words, phrases, sentences, and strategies to participate in class discussions, to show evidence of understanding and express complex concepts in texts, and to express oneself in academic writing.	● Academic vocabulary, according to Calderón, is the centerpiece of *conversational discourse.* ● It connects to *grammar and syntax in context* naturally in that vocabulary is also taught within context. The two dimensions mutually provide meaning for one another.

(Continued)

ALD Dimension	Book Series Summary	Intersections Across Book Series
(Academic Vocabulary)	To enhance academic vocabulary for ELLs and SELs, teachers select words to specifically teach before, during, and after instruction. They select words and phrases that they believe ELLs and SELs need • to know to comprehend the text, • to discuss those concepts, and • to use in their writing later on.	• It connects to *culturally and linguistically responsive practices* in making understandable the distinctions between some common misuses of words ("berry" instead of "very") and the standard English word association.
Grammar and Syntax in Context	As stated in this volume, academic texts pose a particular challenge to ELLs and SELs because they contain technical vocabulary and grammatical structures that are lexically dense and abstract. These include long nominal groups, passives, and complex sentences. • ELLs and SELs need carefully scaffolded instruction to write the academic genres, make the writing cohesive, and use appropriate grammatical structures.	• ELLs and SELs need to be engaged in academic discourse to develop their oral academic language. This provides the base for reading and writing academic texts. • ELLs and SELs also need to develop academic vocabulary, both content specific vocabulary and general academic vocabulary that they can use as they read and write the academic genres. • Teachers should use culturally and linguistically responsive practices that enable students to draw on their full linguistic repertoires.

ALD Dimension	Book Series Summary	Intersections Across Book Series
Culturally and Linguistically Responsive Practices	LeMoine cites Gay (2000) in *defining culturally and linguistically responsive practices* as "ways of knowing, understanding, and representing various ethnic groups in teaching academic subjects, processes, and skills." Its primary features benefitting ELLs and SELs include the following: • Promoting cooperation, collaboration, reciprocity, and mutual responsibility for learning • Incorporating high-status, accurate cultural knowledge about different groups of students • Cultivating the cultural integrity, individual abilities, and academic success of diverse student groups. Simply stated, it is meaningful learning embedded in language and culture.	• Culturally and linguistically responsive practices connect to the development of *academic vocabulary* by providing recognition for prior knowledge and acknowledging culture as part of linguistic development. • It connects to *conversational discourse* by prioritizing cooperative conversation procedures and minimizing confrontational discourse. • It connects to *grammar and syntax in context* by building on second language acquisition strategies and methods (such as SDAIE [Specially Designed Academic Instruction in English]).

standards and expectations. Meaningful and intentional planning around each ALD dimension will allow access for ELLs and SELs into content that might otherwise be inaccessible to them. In the epilogue, you will learn how to use this series in professional development settings and how the book series connects to culturally and linguistically responsive practices.

Epilogue: The Vision

The vision for this book series began with the formation of the Institute for Culturally and Linguistically Responsive Teaching (ICLRT) at Whittier College, the creation of the ICLRT Design Principles, which guide the institute, and the development of an ALD book series, which can assist educators with more deeply meeting the needs of their ELLs and SELs. ICLRT was formed in 2014, and the institute's mission is to "promote relevant research and develop academic resources for ELLs and Standard English Learners (SELs) via linguistically and culturally responsive teaching practices" (ICLRT, n.d.). As such, ICLRT's purpose is to "provide research-based and practitioner-oriented professional development services, tools, and resources for K–12 systems and teacher education programs serving ELLs and SELs." Whittier College is a nationally designated Hispanic-Serving Institution, and ICLRT staff have been providing professional development on ELLs and SELs for more than 15 years, both across California and nationally.

The four books in this ALD series build upon the foundation of the ICLRT Design Principles:

(1) Connecting and addressing the needs of both ELLs and SELs, both linguistically and culturally

(2) Assisting educators with identifying ways to use this book series (and additional ICLRT books) in professional development settings

(3) Addressing the underdeveloped domains of speaking and listening as areas that can be integrated across disciplines and components of ALD

(4) Integrating culturally responsive teaching as a vehicle for honoring both home and primary languages as well as cultural norms for learning

ICLRT Design Principles

Here is a complete list of the ICLRT Design Principles. In parentheses are the books in this series that will address each principle.

(1) **ICLRT believes that the commonalities between ELL and SEL students are more extensive (and more vital to their learning) than the differences between the two groups.**

- ELL and SEL students are at the same end of the learning gap—they often score at the lowest levels on achievement tests. They also rank highly among high school dropouts (*Culture in Context*).
- The academic progress of ELL and SEL students may be hindered by barriers, such as poor identification practices and negative teacher attitudes toward their languages and cultures (*Culture in Context*).
- ELL and SEL students both need specific instructional attention to the development of academic language (*Grammar and Syntax in Context, Conversational Discourse in Context*, and *Vocabulary in Context*).

(2) **ICLRT believes that ongoing, targeted professional development is the key to redirecting teacher attitudes toward ELL and SEL student groups.**

- Teacher knowledge about the histories and cultures of ELL and SEL students can be addressed through professional development and professional learning communities (*Culture in Context*).
- Teachers will become aware of the origins of nonstandard language usage (*Culture in Context*).
- Teachers can become aware of and comfortable with using diverse texts and productive group work to enhance students' sense of belonging (*Conversational Discourse in Context*).
- The ICLRT Academic Language Certification process will provide local demonstration models of appropriate practices and attitudes (*Conversational Discourse in Context*).

(3) **ICLRT believes that ELL and SEL students need to have ongoing, progressive opportunities for listening and speaking throughout their school experiences.**

- The typical ELD sequence of curriculum and courses do not substantially address ELL and SEL student needs for language development (*Conversational Discourse in Context* and *Vocabulary in Context*).
- The ICLRT student shadowing protocol and student shadowing app can provide both quantitative and qualitative information about student speaking and listening (*Conversational Discourse in Context*).
- The ICLRT lesson plan design incorporates appropriate speaking and listening development integrated with reading, writing, and/or content area learning (*Conversational Discourse in Context*).
- Strategies for active listening and academic oral language are embedded in ICLRT's ALD professional development series (*Conversational Discourse in Context*).

(4) **ICLRT believes that its blending of culturally responsive pedagogy (CRP) with ALD will provide teachers of ELL and SEL students with powerful learning tools and strategies.**

- The six characteristics of CRP (Gay, 2000) heighten the already strong effects of solid ALD instruction (*Grammar and Syntax in Context*).
- The storytelling aspects of CRP fit well with the oral language traditions of ELLs and can be used as a foundational tool for both groups to affirm their rich histories (*Culture in Context*).
- Both groups need specific instruction in the four essential components of ALD, including SDAIE strategies (*Grammar and Syntax in Context*, *Conversational Discourse in Context*, and *Vocabulary in Context*).
- The inclusion of CRP and ALD within the ICLRT lesson planning tool makes their use seamless instead of disparate for each group (*Culture in Context*).

Sources: Gay (2000), LeMoine (1999), and Soto-Hinman & Hetzel (2009)

Additional ICLRT Professional Development Resources

This ALD book series is one of the research-based resources developed by ICLRT to assist K–12 systems in serving ELLs and SELs. Other ICLRT resources include the following Corwin texts: *The Literacy Gaps: Building Bridges for ELLs and SELs* (Soto-Hinman & Hetzel, 2009); *ELL Shadowing as a Catalyst for Change* (Soto, 2012); and *Moving From Spoken to Written Language With ELLs* (Soto, 2014). Together, the three books, and their respective professional development modules (available via ICLRT and Corwin), tell a story of how to systemically close achievement gaps with ELLs and SELs by increasing their academic oral language production in academic areas. Specifically, each ICLRT book in the series addresses ALD in the following ways.

- *The Literacy Gaps: Building Bridges for ELLs and SELs* (Soto-Hinman & Hetzel, 2009)—This book is a primer for meeting the literacy needs of ELLs and SELs. Additionally, the linguistic and achievement needs of ELLs and SELs are linked and specific ALD strategies are outlined to comprehensively and coherently meet the needs of both groups of students.
- *ELL Shadowing as a Catalyst for Change* (Soto, 2012)—This book is a way to create urgency around meeting the academic oral language needs of ELLs. Educators shadow an ELL student, guided by the ELL shadowing protocol, which allows them to monitor and collect academic oral language and active listening data. The ethnographic project allows educators to experience a day in the life of an ELL.
- *Moving From Spoken to Written Language With ELLs* (Soto, 2014)—This book assists educators in leveraging spoken language into written language. Specific strategies, such as Think-Pair-Share, the Frayer model, and Reciprocal Teaching, are used to scaffold the writing process, and the Curriculum Cycle (Gibbons, 2002) is recommended as a framework for teaching writing.

Please note that professional development modules for each of the texts listed are also available through ICLRT. For more information, please go to www.whittier.edu/ICLRT.

The ALD book series can be used either after or alongside of *The Literacy Gaps: Building Bridges for ELLs and SELs* (Soto-Hinman & Hetzel, 2009); *ELL Shadowing as a Catalyst for Change* (Soto, 2012); and *Moving From Spoken to Written Language With ELLs* (Soto, 2014) as each book introduces and addresses the importance of ALD for ELLs and SELs. The ALD book series also takes each ALD component deeper by presenting specific research and strategies that will benefit ELLs and SELs in the classroom.

References

Academic Language Development Network. (n.d.). Retrieved from http://aldnetwork.org/

Blythe, T., Allen, D., & Powell, B. S. (1999). *Looking together at student work.* New York: College Teachers Press.

Braddock, R., & Lloyd-Jones, R. (1963). *Research in written composition.* Urbana, IL: National Council of Teachers of English.

Brisk, M. (2015). *Engaging students in academic literacies: Genre-based pedagogy for K–5 classrooms.* New York: Routledge.

Brown, D. (2009). *In other words: Grammar lessons for code-switching, composition, and language study.* Portsmouth, NH: Heinemann.

Brown, H., & Cambourne, B. (1987). *Read and retell.* Portsmouth, NH: Heinemann.

Bunch, G. (2013). Pedagogical language knowledge: Preparing mainstream teachers for English learners in the new standards era. *Review of Educational Research, 37*(February), 298–341.

Calderón, M. (2016). *Academic English mastery: Vocabulary in context.* Thousand Oaks, CA: Corwin.

Chomsky, N. (1965). *Aspects of the theory of syntax.* Cambridge, MA: M.I.T. Press.

Chomsky, N. (1975). *Reflections on language.* New York: Pantheon.

Derewianka, B. (2007). Changing approaches to the conceptualization and teaching of grammar. In J. Cummins & C. Davison (Eds.), *International handbook of English language teaching* (Vol. 2, pp. 843–858). New York: Springer Science+Business Media.

Duksta, L. (2007). *I love you more.* Naperville, IL: Jabberwocky.

Ellis, R. (1998). Teaching and research: Options in grammar teaching. *TESOL Quarterly, 32*(1), 39–60.

Fang, Z. (2004). Scientific literacy: A systemic functional linguistics perspective. *Wiley InterScience, 89*(2), 335–347. doi:10.1002/sce.20050

Fang, Z. (2008). Going beyond the fab five: Helping students cope with the unique linguistic challenges of expository reading in the middle grades. *Journal of Adolescent and Adult Literacy, 51*(6), 476–487.

Fisher, D., Rothenberg, C., & Frey, N. (2007). *Language learners in the English classroom*. Urbana, IL: National Council of Teachers of English.

Freeman, D., & Freeman, Y. (2009). *Academic language for English language learners and struggling readers: How to help students succeed across content areas*. Portsmouth, NH: Heinemann.

Freeman, D., & Freeman, Y. (2014). *Essential linguistics: What teachers need to know to teach ESL, reading, spelling, and grammar*. Portsmouth, NH: Heinemann.

Gay, G. (2000). *Culturally responsive teaching: Theory, research, and practice*. New York: Teachers College Press.

Gibbons, P. (2002). *Scaffolding language, scaffolding learning: Teaching second language learners in the mainstream classroom*. Portsmouth, NH: Heinemann.

Gibbons, P. (2009). *English learners, academic literacy, and thinking: Learning in the challenge zone*. Portsmouth, NH: Heinemann.

Gibbons, P. (2014). *Scaffolding language: Scaffolding learning* (2nd ed.). Portsmouth, NH: Heinemann.

Grosjean, F. (2010). *Bilingualism: Life and reality*. Cambridge, MA: Harvard University Press.

Halliday, M. (1989). *Spoken and written language*. Oxford: Oxford University Press.

Halliday, M. A. K. (1994). *An introduction to functional grammar* (2nd ed.). London: Edward Arnold.

Institute for Culturally and Linguistically Responsive Teaching (ICLRT). (n.d.). Retrieved from http://www.whittier.edu/ICLRT

James, H. (1902). *The wings of the dove*. New York: Charles Scribner's Sons.

Krashen, S. (1982). *Principles and practice in second language acquisition*. New York: Pergamon Press.

Krashen, S. (1992). *Fundamentals of language education*. Torrance, CA: Laredo.

Krashen, S. (1998). Teaching grammar: Why bother? *California English, 3*(3), 8.

Krashen, S., & Terrell, T. (1983). *The Natural Approach: Language acquisition in the classroom*. Hayward, CA: Alemany.

Larsen-Freeman, D. (1986). *Techniques and principles in language teaching* (R. Campbell, Ed.). Oxford: Oxford University Press.

LeMoine, N., & L. A. Unified School District. (1999). *English for your success: A language development program for African American students. Handbook of successful strategies for educators*. NJ: The Peoples Publishing Group.

Long, E. (2004). *Mañana iguana*. New York: Holliday House.

Long, M. (2001). Focus on form: A design feature in language teaching methodology. In C. Candlin & N. Mercer (Eds.), *English language teaching in its social context: A reader* (pp. 180–190). London: Routledge.

Macauley, W. J. (1947). The difficulty of grammar. *British Journal of Educational Psychology, 17*, 153–162.

MacDonald, R., Boals, T., Castro, M., Cook, G., Lundberg, T., & White, P. (2015). *Formative language assessment for English learners*. Portsmouth, NH: Heinemann.

McLaughlin, C., Thompson, M., & Zike, D. (2002). *Integrated physics and chemistry*. Columbus, OH: Glencoe/McGraw-Hill.

Migration Policy Institute Tabulation of Data From the United Nations, Department of Economic and Social Affairs. (2013). Trends in international migrant stock: Migrants by origin and destination, 2013 revision (United Nations database, POP/DB/MIG/Stock/Rev.2013). Retrieved from http://esa.un.org/unmigration/TIMSO2013/migrantstocks2013.htm

Randell, B., Giles, J., & Smith, A. (1996). *Mom*. Crystal Lake, IL: Rigby.

Soto, I. (2012). *ELL shadowing as a catalyst for change*. Thousand Oaks, CA: Corwin.

Soto, I. (2014). *From spoken to written language with ELLs*. Thousand Oaks, CA: Corwin.

Soto-Hinman, I., & Hetzel, J. (2009). *The literacy gaps: Building bridges for ELLs and SELs*. Thousand Oaks, CA: Corwin.

Schleppegrell, M. J. (2004). *The language of schooling: A functional linguistics perspective*. Mahwah, NJ: Lawrence Erlbaum.

Weaver, C. (1996). *Teaching grammar in context*. Portsmouth, NH: Boynton/Cook.

Wong-Fillmore, L. (2013). Defining academic language. *Education Week*. Retrieved rom http://www.edweek.org/ew/articles/2013/10/30/10cc-academiclanguage.h33.html

Zwiers, J. (2016). *Academic English mastery: Conversational skills in context*. Thousand Oaks, CA: Corwin.

Index

IS YOUR ACADEMIC LANGUAGE MASTERY LIBRARY COMPLETE?

Academic Language Mastery: Conversational Discourse in Context
Jeff Zwiers and Ivannia Soto

Here, Jeff Zwiers reveals the power of academic conversation in helping students develop language, clarify concepts, comprehend complex texts, and fortify thinking and relational skills. With this book as your road map, you'll learn how to

- Foster the skills and language students must develop for productive interactions
- Implement strategies for scaffolding conversations between students
- Formatively assess students' oral language development

Academic Language Mastery: Vocabulary in Context
Margarita Calderón and Ivannia Soto

Vocabulary instruction is not an end in itself. Instead, academic words are best taught as tools for completing and constructing more complex messages. Look to renowned author Margarita Calderón for expert guidelines on how to

- Teach high-frequency academic words and discipline-specific vocabulary across content areas
- Utilize strategies for teaching academic vocabulary, moving students from Tier 1 to Tiers 2 and 3 words and selecting appropriate words to teach
- Assess vocabulary development as you go

Academic Language Mastery: Culture in Context
Noma LeMoine and Ivannia Soto

Never underestimate the critical role culture and language play in our students' education. In this volume, Noma LeMoine offers new insight on how culturally and linguistically responsive pedagogy validates, facilitates, liberates, and empowers our diverse students. Learn how to

- Implement instructional strategies designed to meet the linguistic and cultural needs of ELLs and SELs
- Use language variation as an asset in the classroom
- Recognize and honor prior knowledge, home languages, and cultures

CORWIN

A SAGE Publishing Company

CORWIN HAS ONE MISSION: to enhance education through intentional professional learning.

We build long-term relationships with our authors, educators, clients, and associations who partner with us to develop and continuously improve the best evidence-based practices that establish and support lifelong learning.

Solutions you want. Experts you trust. Results you need.

AUTHOR CONSULTING

Author Consulting

On-site professional learning with sustainable results! Let us help you design a professional learning plan to meet the unique needs of your school or district. www.corwin.com/pd

INSTITUTES

Institutes

Corwin Institutes provide collaborative learning experiences that equip your team with tools and action plans ready for immediate implementation. www.corwin.com/institutes

ECOURSES

eCourses

Practical, flexible online professional learning designed to let you go at your own pace. www.corwin.com/ecourses

READ2EARN

Read2Earn

Did you know you can earn graduate credit for reading this book? Find out how: www.corwin.com/read2earn

Contact an account manager at (800) 831-6640 or visit **www.corwin.com** for more information.